The Making of Pakistan

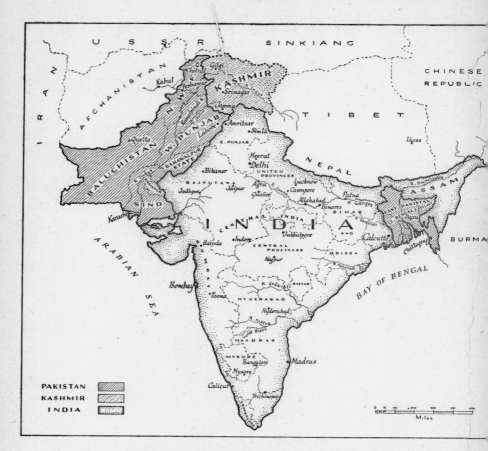

GENERAL MAP OF INDIA AND PAKISTAN

To

MY WIFE

Preface

Although most of the statements in Part I of this book can be supported by references, which are listed in a short bibliography, in Part II—the examination of Pakistan as it is today—I have had to rely largely on information supplied verbally, on unpublished material kindly made available by the Pakistan and Provincial Governments and by non-officials, and on my own observation.

I wish to record my appreciation of the courtesy and frankness of all who found time to see me in Pakistan; of H.E. the Governor General, and of ministers and officers of the Pakistan Government; of the Prime Minister, ministers and officers of the Governments of East Bengal, Sind, and the North West Frontier Province, of the Chief Secretary and officers of the West Punjab Government; of the representatives of the Muslim League, of the Hindu, Scheduled Caste and Christian minorities, as well as of non-official organizations; and of many private individuals.

In England I have greatly benefited from the kindness of Professor Sir Reginald Coupland and of Mr. Guy Wint, both of whom read the manuscript, and from the advice and help of the Librarian and staff of the Indian Institute at Oxford. Mr. Salman Ali, Pakistan Press Attaché in London, and Sirdar Khaswant Singh, Indian Press Attaché in London, have also kindly provided me with useful material. Above all, I acknowledge my indebtedness to my wife, but for whom the book could not have been completed.

None of the above has, of course, any responsibility for what I have written.

9

Preface

I have been fortunate in persuading Professor Ahmed Ali of Karachi to contribute an essay on 'The Culture of Pakistan', a subject on which I was not competent to write. Professor Ahmed Ali is perhaps best known in England as the author of the novel *Twilight in Delhi*. In Pakistan he is widely known for his delightful translations of Urdu, as well as of Chinese and Indonesian, poetry. Professor Ahmed Ali and I wrote separately, one in Karachi and the other in Oxford, and neither of us can therefore necessarily be held to share the views or conclusions of the other.

In any discussion of the origin and nature of Pakistan, some delicate ground has to be covered. In traversing this, I may be considered by the reader to have been biased by some particular experience. It seems, therefore, only fair to state what my acquaintanceship with the Indo-Pakistan subcontinent has been. From 1942–4 I served with the Friends Ambulance Unit, India Section. From 1944–5 I was Deputy Director of Relief and Rehabilitation to the Government of Bengal. During the Punjab disturbances of 1947 I worked with the Friends Relief Service, mostly in the evacuation of non-Muslims from Western Pakistan; and from June 1948 until April 1949 was a member of the Secretariat of the United Nations Commission for India and Pakistan, which was mediating in the Kashmir dispute. On leaving the staff of the Commission in 1949, I made a tour of Pakistan as a private individual to gather information for this book. None of the material which is contained in it was obtained in an official capacity.

In writing of Pakistan's relations with India, I have tried to avoid any comment which might exacerbate the unhappy relations between the two countries, and to confine myself to narrating the events as they occurred. I have had the privilege of making many friends on both sides of the border, and if anything which I have written causes offence I trust they will realize that it is not intended.

RICHARD SYMONDS

Oxford, November 1949.

Contents

Maps

Introduction

The Dominion of Pakistan which came into existence in August 1947 has an estimated population of eighty millions. It is thus the fifth largest nation in the world; is the largest Muslim nation; and has more inhabitants than the combined 'white' part of the British Commonwealth. If size alone does not justify a study of Pakistan, it has other characteristics of unusual interest. Geographically, it consists of two separate areas divided by a thousand miles of foreign territory. Politically, it is a state which has been deliberately created not on an economic, linguistic or racial basis, but on that of religious unity.

The bibliography of Pakistan in England and America is extraordinarily scanty. An admirable pamphlet, published by the British Commonwealth Relations Office in 1949, advises the reader on half a dozen books on each Dominion and colony, but is unable to mention one on Pakistan.[1] Moreover, of those who watched the evolution of Pakistan with greatest interest, most were opposed to it, and almost all regarded it as impracticable.

Thus Pandit Nehru, whose *Autobiography* is still perhaps the most widely read book on India in Britain and the U.S.A., wrote in 1936:

'The Muslim nation in India—a nation within a nation, and not even compact, but vague, spread out, indeterminate. Politically the idea is absurd. Economically it is fantastic; it is hardly worth considering. . . . This idea of a Muslim nation is the figment of a few imaginations only, and but for the publicity given

---

[1] *Origins and Purpose—A Handbook on the Commonwealth of Nations,* London, H.M. Stationery Office, 1949.

13

Introduction

it by the Press few people would have heard of it. And even if many people believed in it, it would still vanish at the touch of reality.'[1]

Nehru, of course, as a Congressman, believed in the unity of India almost as an article of faith. His estimate in the 'thirties, moreover, was shared by Muslim leaders who later were among the founders of Pakistan, such as the representatives of the Muslim League and Muslim Conference who told the Joint Select Committee of Parliament in 1933 that Pakistan was 'only a students' scheme', 'chimerical and unpracticable'. But even in the 'forties, after the adoption of Pakistan as the objective of the Muslim League, most British writers were strongly opposed to it.

The Left, influenced partly by personal links with the Congress, are most emphatically on record against the creation of Pakistan. Thus Edward Thompson[2] in 1940 did not 'believe in the . . . solution of Pakistan. . . . Can any sound state be created except along the line of strong national boundaries? It is a myth, our belief that the seventy millions of Indian Muslims are solidly against Congress and Dominion status.' R. Palme Dutt in the same year wrote: 'The communal issue is grossly misrepresented in the official Press and has given rise to genuine misconceptions on the part of progressive and sympathetic elements in Britain, largely because the impression has spread that the Muslim League may be regarded as representing the eighty million Muslims of India. The claim is fictitious and has only to be tested by the evidence to be exploded. . . . The attempted artificial division of the single Indian people into two nations can never be and will never be accepted by the national movement.'[3] H. N. Brailsford in 1943 wrote that 'to erect once again a cactus hedge across the peninsula would be a crime against civilization'.[4] The Rev. Reginald Sorensen, M.P., one of India's best

[1] Jawarharlal Nehru, *Autobiography*, London, 1936, p. 469.
[2] Edward Thompson, *Enlist India for Freedom*, London, 1940, p. 58 ff. Though Thompson was not a party man, his book was published by Gollancz in a series of left-wing pamphlets.
[3] R. Palme Dutt, *India Today*, London, 1940, p. 420.
[4] H. N. Brailsford, *Subject India*, London, 1943, p. 92.

Introduction

friends in the Labour Party, considered as late as 1947 that Pakistan was 'impossible as well as undesirable'.[1]

The Right, being until 1945 more directly concerned with the administration of India, was more cautious. Even so, L. S. Amery, who was Secretary of State for India at the time, in 1941 saw 'insuperable objections' to Pakistan.[2] Administrators and scholars were also doubtful. R. G. Casey, who had been Governor of Bengal from 1944–6, concluded that the establishment of Pakistan would be followed by a tariff war with India, in which the latter would prevail, and that Pakistan would not have sufficient international credit to raise loans.[3] Even Sir Reginald Coupland, who made much the most careful and objective study of Pakistan before it came into being, drew among others two conclusions which have not so far been entirely justified, that the heavy cost of defence in Pakistan would cause a fall in the standard of living, and that a large scale exchange of population with India would be impossible.[4]

Nor were American writers more prescient than the British. Mr. John Gunther in 1939 considered that Jinnah had 'all but ruined his position by adopting a fierce separatism'.[5] Miss Kate Mitchell, writing in 1943, was frankly hostile to the Muslim League and to the idea of Pakistan.[6] Robert Aura Smith of the *New York Times*, in a detailed study of the political events of 1946–7, believed that if Pakistan were created, its foreign policy would be dictated from Cairo.[7]

Yet Pakistan came into existence, and after two years has a balanced budget, a favourable balance of trade, a stable government, an independent foreign policy, and a standard of living at least as high as that of her neighbours.

It would not indeed be necessary to recollect the predictions

[1] R. Sorensen, *My Impressions of India*, London, 1947.
[2] L. S. Amery, *India and Freedom*, London, 1944, p. 87.
[3] R. G. Casey, *An Australian in India*, London, 1947, p. 79.
[4] R. Coupland, *India: A Restatement*, Oxford, 1945, p. 261.
[5] John Gunther, *Inside Asia*, London, 1939, p. 510.
[6] Kate Mitchell, *India, An American View*, New York, 1944.
[7] Robert Aura Smith, *Divided India*, New York, 1947, p. 180.

Introduction

of disaster, if it were not that they are remembered in Pakistan itself. The Pakistanis believe, as can be plainly seen in their newspapers and in the speeches of their leaders, that British public opinion, and in particular Labour Party opinion, is prejudiced against them. They have a dangerous sense of being ignored and taken for granted at a time when India and Pakistan, themselves bitterly opposed, are in the immediate path of advancing Communism.

This book is written in the hope that it may help to dispel that feeling by promoting a wider knowledge and understanding of Pakistan in Britain and America. Part I is concerned with the question 'How and why did Pakistan come into being?' Part II endeavours to answer the question 'What is Pakistan?' A fuller work cannot be written for several years, for most of the memoirs and many of the official documents of the period immediately preceding and following the creation of Pakistan are yet unpublished. In the meantime, if this book serves to stimulate further study, its object will have been achieved.

Part I
THE GROWTH OF A NATION

CHAPTER I

The Muslims in India

*Arabs in Sind—Northern Invaders—The Mogul Empire
and its Decline—The Muslims after the Mutiny*

The earliest Muslims to come to India may have sailed from Arabia in the lifetime of the Prophet Muhammad. For centuries Arab traders and sailors had been familiar with the ports of Western India. Some of them settled there, and it even seems that certain rajas of Madras, whose prosperity depended on the maritime trade, encouraged some of their youthful subjects to become Mussalmans and grow up to understand navigation.[1] The descendants of these Arabs and their converts are still to be found on the Malabar coast.

The Prophet, after early years of persecution, died in A.D. 632, a ruler who united in his person civil and military, as well as religious, authority. The successors to that authority, the consecutive Caliphs of Medina, Damascus and Baghdad, used it to send out armies to conquer much of the then known world. In the time of the Damascus Caliphate the Governor of Basra heard that one of his ships had been looted at Debul in Sind, and sent a punitive expedition under the leadership of Muhammad Bin Qasim to avenge the insult in A.D. 712. This earliest Muslim invasion of India resulted in the conquest and conversion of most of Sind. The authority of the Caliphate was withdrawn from Sind in the ninth century, but the majority of its inhabitants

[1] *Malabar District Gazetteer*, 1908, p. 190.

19

have remained Muslims under successive rulers until the present day.

The wider introduction of Islam into India was to come not from the west but the north. Between A.D. 999 and 1025 the Sultan Mahmud of Ghazni in Afghanistan made seventeen raids into Indian territory. In the course of them he conquered and annexed the Punjab. Mahmud was impelled both by loot and piety. He 'demolished idol temples and established Islam. He captured cities, killed the polluted wretches, destroying the idolators, and gratifying Muslims.'[1] His successors, however, lost their possessions both in Ghazni and India to the rival Turkish dynasty of Ghur, which, defeating the Rajput hero Prithviraj, established a Muslim kingdom in Delhi in 1192.

Five Turkish or Afghan dynasties, usually known as the 'Pathan Kings', ruled at Delhi from 1192 to 1526. Their dominion extended over the whole of Northern India, but they never successfully subdued the south. It was in this period that the present communal map of the subcontinent took its shape. The earlier Turco-Afghans, more fanatical than the Arabs in Sind, appear to have acted on the principle that the Hindus, not being 'people of the Book', that is people worshipping a single god, could only be offered the alternatives of Islam or the sword. In time, however, the Hindus acquired the rights of 'dhimmis', that is of persons who, while retaining their own religion, purchased protection and immunity from military service by payment of a poll tax.

Nor must it be concluded that the spread of Islam in India was entirely, or even mainly, due to fear. The armies were accompanied by, often preceded by, intrepid missionaries. Many Muslim saints and scholars migrated to Northern India when Central Asia was invaded by the Moguls. 'These holy men would seem to have set themselves seriously to convert to Islam the remaining Hindu agriculturists and pagans of this part of India, and it is to their persuasion rather than the sword that

[1] Al Utbi, quoted in Ambedkar *Pakistan*.

The Muslims in India

the people of West Punjab owe their faith in Islam.'[1] The religion which the missionaries brought made a striking appeal to the lower castes of Hinduism. Whole occupational groups, doomed under their existing religion to perpetual subordination, became willing converts. Thus, right up to the time of the Partition of India in 1947, the overwhelming majority of leather workers, butchers, weavers and tailors were Muslims. In East Bengal in particular, where more than half the present population of Pakistan now live, the appeal was irresistible.

'To these poor people—fishermen, hunters, pirates and low-caste tillers of the soil—Islam came as a revelation from on high. It was the creed of the ruling race; its missionaries were men of zeal who brought the gospel of the unity of God and the equality of men in his sight to a despised and neglected population.'[2]

The circumstances of Bengal were exceptional. The mild rule of Buddhism had only recently been replaced there by Hinduism when the missionaries of Islam came. In general, the invaders settled and made converts in the lands which they first came to —the present Punjab and North West Frontier Provinces. For the rest, the Muslim settlements were mainly along the major lines of communication, and Islam never penetrated widely into Central or Southern India. Moreover, the vanquished exercised a subtle and profound influence on the victors. The invaders had brought no women, and, marrying Hindus, married some of their customs with them. The converts, imperfectly understanding their new creed, deified the Pirs who had converted them, and worshipped their relics. Muslim religious processions in remote places took on the character of Hindu car festivals. There were even, as can be seen from modern census reports, lapses into hereditary castes. As Iqbal said: 'We have outhindued the Hindu himself: we are suffering from a double caste system—the religious caste system, sectarianism and the social caste system, which we have either learnt or inherited from the Hindus.'

[1] Sir E. McLagan in *District Gazetteer of Multan*, 1902, p. 37.
[2] W. W. Hunter, Article on 'The Religions of India', London *Times*, Feb. 25, 1888, quoted in Arnold, *The Preaching of Islam*, p. 279.

The Muslims in India

Culturally, the blend of the Islamic with the Hindu influence had much to commend it. The Indo-Saracenic architectural style is still the most graceful to be seen in the subcontinent. For the Turks indeed, Persia remained the cultural home, and Persian the literary language. But Hindustani, a combination of Persian with the Hindi spoken round Delhi, became gradually the lingua franca not only of the army but of Northern India, whether written in the Urdu (Persian) script or in Sanskrit characters.

To the Turco-Afghans succeeded the Moguls, under whose first six emperors (1526–1707) Indian Muslims look back to their period of glory. The Moguls were Turco-Mongols from Central Asia. The first conqueror, Babar, was ruler of a petty kingdom in Turkestan. His easy victory over the last of the Turco-Afghan dynasties, the Lodis, was mainly due to his superior artillery. The Moguls laid the foundations of the modern administration of India and the magnificence of their buildings remains one of the marvels of the world. But for an understanding of the evolution of Pakistan it is necessary to consider more especially their religious policy, and in particular that of the two emperors among them whose names are most remembered in India and Pakistan today.

Akbar (1556–1605) subdued the whole subcontinent except the extreme south and ruled over Afghanistan also. His regular assessment of agricultural revenue placed the empire's economy on a sound basis. From the outset of his reign he determined that his power should rest not merely on the precarious authority of Mongols, Turks and Afghans, but on the broader loyalty of all his subjects, of whatever race or religion. He obtained the support of the leading Rajput chieftains by confirming them in their estates and by marriage alliances. He prohibited the levy of taxes on Hindu pilgrims, and the collection of the Jizya, the differential tax claimed from non-Muslims. Cow slaughter became illegal. Hindus were employed as ministers and generals, and his city of Fatehpur Sikri remains a remarkable synthesis of Hindu and Mogul styles. In the latter part of his reign, after lengthy debates with Islamic, Hindu and Christian divines, he founded a new religion, with himself as its sole authoritative exponent, no doubt hoping thus to unite all his subjects in a common faith.

Hindu and most British historians have found Akbar the greatest and most enlightened of the Moguls. By some Muslim historians, however, he is depicted as a renegade who caused mosques to be used as warehouses and bandstands; who forbade any child to be named 'Muhammad'; and who proclaimed that 'any opposition on the part of his subjects to an order passed by His Majesty shall involve damnation in the world to come'.

Aurungzeb (1658–1707) was the last of the Great Moguls, and in many ways of tougher moral fibre than any of them, industrious, self-controlled and deeply religious. His purpose was to organize the empire in strict accordance with the laws of Islam. In the course of this, according to Hindu historians, customs duties were differentiated in favour of Muslims; the Jizya tax was reimposed on non-Muslims; temples were destroyed; and Hindus were barred from high office. Muslim historians,[1] however, maintain that his policy has been distorted by Hindus: that the Jizya tax was a generous measure allowing non-Muslims to buy exemption from military service; that the additional two and a half per cent customs duty payable by Hindus was to compensate for the compulsory poor rate, payable by Muslims only; that he protected Islam indeed from the anti-Islamic policy initiated by Akbar, but that when asked to dismiss non-Muslims in his service he wrote: 'Religion has no concern with secular business, and in matters of this kind bigotry has no place.'

Aurungzeb spent much of his life fighting against Hindu chieftains, Rajputs and Marathas, and his reign ended in economic ruin. Yet the subsequent collapse of the empire cannot solely be attributed to the effective guerrilla tactics of the Marathas. A more fundamental reason for the decline was the lack of

[1] On both Akbar and Aurungzeb, Moreland and Chatterjee's *Short History of India*, and Sir J. N. Sarkar's *History of Aurungzeb*, may be compared with Faruki's *Aurungzeb* for typically contrasted accounts.

fixed rules as to the imperial succession. On the death of each emperor there was fratricidal war until the strongest claimant exterminated his rivals. After Aurungzeb's death there was never a claimant strong enough to win and hold the whole empire. Similarly, the Mogul nobility's rights were not hereditary, and thus the military machine in which they were the most important link was too loose to stand up to continuous strain.

Just as Aurungzeb's character has been a subject of controversy, so has that of his most effective enemy, the Maratha Shivaji. In Western India he has remained a legendary chivalrous cavalry leader. To most Muslim writers, on the other hand, he is a treacherous freebooter. In the Mogul period more than any other, if it is true that Hindus and Muslims have a common history, their interpretations of it have caused more discord than harmony.

The death of Aurungzeb was followed by the disintegration of the Mogul Empire. In Western and Central India the Maratha power could no longer be effectively disputed. The sack of Delhi by Persian invaders in 1739, and the increasing strength of British, French and Dutch settlements on the coasts left the emperor little more than moral authority and sentimental appeal. There were indeed substantial Muslim successor states. In the south, the Nizam in Hyderabad, Haidar Ali and his son Tippoo in Mysore. In the north, the Nawab of Bengal controlled most of Bengal and Bihar, and there were independent Nawabs of Oudh and Rohilkhand. But as soon as the British East India Company had disposed of its European rivals, it inexorably absorbed both Hindu and Muslim states. The Nawab of Bengal was defeated by Clive in 1757. Rohilkhand was merged in Oudh through British intervention in 1774. Tippoo was defeated and killed by Wellesley in 1799. Delhi was occupied in 1803, though its powerless emperor lived on in the Red Fort. Sind, nominally subordinate to Afghanistan but governed by its own Ameers, was annexed almost accidentally in the course of the Afghan War of 1843. The Punjab, also occupied by the Afghans in the eighteenth century, first fell to the Sikhs and was annexed by the

The Muslims in India

Company in 1849. By 1850 only Oudh and Hyderabad remained Muslim states of consequence. The annexation of the former by Dalhousie was a not inconsiderable factor in causing Muslims to rise against the Company in the Mutiny. The loyalty of the Nizam to the British at that time, however, enabled Hyderabad to remain, under British suzerainty, the leading princely state of India until the Partition of 1947.

The responsibility of the Muslims for the Indian Mutiny of 1857 and the extent of their participation in it was considerably exaggerated by contemporary British historians and diarists. This was not unnatural, as the mutineers made the last aged Mogul emperor their figurehead in Delhi. Moreover, the activities of the Wahabis, reformists preaching that no Muslim could be loyal to a non-Muslim ruler, had attracted the attention of many of the Company's servants in the first half of the century. A recent British estimate is likely to be more accurate.

'Of the fifty million Muslims in India, scarcely three out of every ten thousand can have rallied to their restored emperor . . .

'There is no evidence to suggest that the restoration of Bahadur Shah was part of an organized Muslim plot. Firoz Shah, the most enterprising member of his household, was in Persia when the Mutiny began and returned only to lead some revolted soldiery from Indore and Gwalior. Khan Bahadur Khan, a government pensioner, set himself up as a viceroy at Bareilly and established Mohammedan rule in Rohilkhand. Apart from these two, few Mohammedans of any standing were openly against the Government.'[1]

Yet, if the Mutiny unreasonably and disastrously hardened British feeling against the Muslims, this was only the final stage in their political, cultural and economic decline, which had commenced in the middle of the previous century.

Under the Moguls and in those Muslim states which succeeded to part of their dominions, the Muslims had filled the great majority of the higher posts in the army, the administration and

[1] Edward Thompson and G. T. Garratt in the *Rise and Fulfilment of British Rule in India*, pp. 436, 443.

25

the learned professions. The East India Company had no use
for either Muslims or Hindus in senior positions in its service. It
did need a multitude of subordinate officials, but they had to be
English speaking. In 1835, as a result of Macaulay's famous
Minute, English replaced Persian as the official language of
higher education. The Hindus were quick to take advantage of
the schools opened by the British missionaries, who began to
come to India in the evangelical movement of the early nineteenth century. They were indeed encouraged by their leaders to
do so. The Muslim centres of learning, Delhi and Lucknow,
were far from the British centres of government, education and
commerce at Calcutta, Bombay and Madras. Muslim religious
leaders were suspicious of Christian schools. The old traditions
lingered on in Lucknow, capital of Oudh, where the King had
a library of two hundred thousand books and manuscripts and
where the Urdu literature of the period was 'full of joy and
pride'.[1] But Lucknow and Delhi were sacked in the Mutiny, and
only in faraway Hyderabad did the old culture continue in a
living form. Sir William Hunter, in a remarkable book published
shortly after the Mutiny, gives a striking picture of the decaying
Muslim middle class in Bengal. They had lost their traditional
positions in the police, courts of law, magistracy, army and
revenue offices. Of 240 Indian pleaders admitted to the Calcutta
bar between 1852 and 1868 only one was a Muslim. There were
no Muslim covenanted officers or High Court judges. In all the
government-gazetted appointments of the province, they filled
only 92 places out of 1,338. 'The proportion of the race which
a century ago had the monopoly of the Government has now
fallen to less than one twenty-third of the whole administrative
body.'

Hunter concludes with a warning to his countrymen.

'There is no use shutting our ears to the fact that the Indian
Muhammedans arraign us on a list of charges as serious as have
ever been brought against a government. . . . They accuse us
of having closed every honourable walk of life to the professors

[1] A. Yusuf Ali in *Modern India and the West*, p. 397.

of their creed. They accuse us of having introduced a system of education which leaves their whole community unprovided for, and which landed it in contempt and beggary. They accuse us of having brought misery into thousands of families by abolishing their law officers, who gave the sanction of religion to marriage, and who from time immemorial have been the depositories and administrators of the Domestic Law of Islam. They accuse us of imperilling their souls by denying them the means of performing the duties of their faith. Above all, they charge us with deliberate malversation of their religious foundations, and with misappropriation on the largest scale of their educational funds.'[1]

[1] W. W. Hunter, *Indian Mussalmans*, p. 145.

CHAPTER II

The Muslim Renaissance

Syed Ahmed—Ameer Ali—Iqbal

No single individual had a greater responsibility for the recovery of Muslim political influence after the Mutiny and for the adjustment of the Indian Muslims to Western ideas than Sir Syed Ahmed Khan.

SYED AHMED was born in 1817 of a Delhi family traditionally in the Mogul service. He himself entered the service of the East India Company and became a judge in Delhi. In the Mutiny he was responsible for saving many European lives and was decorated by the Government. In 1858 he wrote in Urdu a thoughtful pamphlet on the Mutiny, the most significant cause of which he stated to be the British ignorance of the Indian mind. He suggested that this should be remedied by Indian representation in the Viceroy's Legislative Council. In another pamphlet, *The Loyal Mohammedans of India,* he defended his co-religionists against British charges of disloyalty. In 1869, at the age of fifty-two, he visited England for the first time, and his impressions profoundly influenced his subsequent public life.

'Without flattering the English,' he wrote home from London, 'I can truly say that the natives of India, high and low, merchants and petty shopkeepers, educated and illiterate, when contrasted with the English in education, manners and uprightness, are as like them as a dirty animal is to an able and upright man. The English have every reason to believe us in India to be imbecile brutes.'[1]

[1] Graham, *Sir Syed Ahmed Khan,* p. 125.

28

The Muslim Renaissance

He returned to India convinced that the only hope for the advancement of his community was by the absorption of Western learning and science, and by reconciliation with the British. He spent much time and effort justifying this step theologically, showing that Islam was compatible with Victorian values and ideals; and founded an Urdu journal modelled on the *Spectator* and the *Tatler*. But his greatest contribution to the Muslim recovery was the establishment of the Muhammadan Anglo-Oriental College (subsequently Aligarh University) in 1875.

Syed Ahmed had found that the greatest objections which his contemporaries had to sending their sons to government colleges were the absence of Islamic education in those colleges and the danger that the boys' faith might be corrupted in them. Yet unless young Muslims could obtain an English education they were barred from advancement in any branch of government service and seriously handicapped in commerce. To overcome these objections, Syed Ahmed created in Aligarh a college where, although the teaching was in English and the main curriculum Western, both the Arabic language and religious instruction were compulsory subjects. The college was residential, on the Oxford and Cambridge model, and its first three principals were Englishmen. Syed Ahmed realized that his own advanced theological views had aroused the suspicions of many Muslims, and he therefore made it clear that he would have no personal responsibility for the religious curriculum.

The patronage of Aligarh by the Nizam of Hyderabad and the Amir of Afghanistan satisfied the scruples of Muslim parents. The presence of the Viceroy and the Governor of the province at the college's annual ceremonies made it certain that its graduates would be welcomed in government service. And the names of the Maharajahs of Patiala and Vizianagram on the subscription lists cleared it of any suspicion of being narrowly communalist.

The college was successful in Syed Ahmed's immediate objective of producing not only candidates for the higher ranks of government service, but political leaders as capable as the

The Muslim Renaissance

Hindus. Maulana Mohamed Ali, leader of the Khilafat Movement, Khwaja Nazimuddin, the present Governor General, and Liaquat Ali, Prime Minister of Pakistan, were all Aligarh men. But its wider influence was even more important. The distinctive outward mark of the Aligarh man, a modified form of European dress with a red fez, symbolized a desire for social reform combined with a staunch loyalty to his religion which he carried with him throughout Muslim India.

Syed Ahmed retired from government service in 1876, was knighted, and sat as a member of the Governor General's Legislative Council from 1878–83. His most notable action in this capacity was his successful insistence that Muslims should receive separate nomination to the local self-government institutions which were created by Lord Ripon. His speech on this occasion deserves to be quoted at some length not only for its influence on the course of events but on subsequent Muslim political thought.

'The system of representation by election means the representation of the views and interests of the majority of the population, and in countries where the population is composed of one race and one creed it is no doubt the best system that can be adopted. But, my lord, in a country like India, where caste distinctions still flourish, where there is no fusion of the various races, where religious distinctions are still violent, where education in its modern sense has not made an equal or proportionate progress among all the sections of the population, I am convinced that the introduction of the principle of election, pure and simple, for representation of various interests on the local boards and district councils would be attended with evils of greater significance than purely economic considerations. So long as differences of race and creed, and the distinctions of caste form an important element in the socio-political life of India, and influence her inhabitants in matters connected with the administration and welfare of the country at large, the system of election, pure and simple, cannot be safely adopted. The larger community would totally override the interests of the smaller community, and the ignorant public would hold Government responsible for introducing measures which might make the differences of race and creed more violent than ever.'[1]

Towards the end of Syed Ahmed's life, the Indian National Congress was founded. Although the Congress was entirely loyal to the Government in its early years, it pressed for an increase in representative government for India and a wider recruitment of Indians for government service by open competitive examination. Syed Ahmed strongly opposed the Congress's demands and Muslim participation in them. His speeches on the subject at Lucknow and Meerut in 1887–8 have great interest for the student of Pakistan.[2]

Partly, indeed, his opposition to the extension of representative government and to recruitment by competitive examination was aristocratic.

'Men of good family would never like to trust their lives and property to people of low rank, with whose humble origins they are well acquainted.'

But his main theme was: 'If in your opinion the peoples of India do form one nation, then no doubt competitive examination may be introduced. . . . Have the Mohammedans attained to such a position as regards higher English education which is necessary for higher appointments as to put them on a level with Hindus or not? Most certainly not.

'The proposals of the Congress are exceedingly inexpedient for a country which is inhabited by two different nations. . . . Now suppose that all the English . . . were to leave India . . . then who would be rulers of India? Is it possible that under these circumstances two nations—the Mohammedan and Hindu—could sit on the same throne and remain equal in power? Most certainly not. It is necessary that one of them should conquer the other and thrust it down. To hope that both could remain equal is to desire the impossible and the inconceivable.'

[1] Speech in Governor General's Council, 12th January 1883. Text in Coupland, *Indian Problem*, part i, appendix ii.
[2] Sir Syed Ahmed, *The Present State of Indian Politics*.

The Muslim Renaissance

The wisest course for the Muslims, therefore, 'behindhand in education and deficient in wealth', was to educate themselves and quietly assert themselves in commerce. 'When you have fully acquired education, then you will know what rights you can legitimately demand of the British Government.' In the meantime, they must refuse to support the Hindus in their demands for representative government: they would be amply rewarded for their loyalty and for their educational effort by positions in government service.

Syed Ahmed died in 1898. In theology he had reconciled Islam with Western learning. In education he had given the Muslims their own college where they could pursue Western studies without becoming worse Muslims. In government service and commerce he had made openings for the new educated Muslim middle class. In politics he had stated that the Muslims were a nation who could not and must not be submerged in a system of government by majority vote. The Pakistanis rightly claim him as one of the fathers of their country.

AMEER ALI. One aspect of the relative contributions of Syed Ahmed and of Ameer Ali to the Indian Muslim revival has been well summarized:

'Sir Syed . . . had maintained that Islam was not inimical to progress. Ameer Ali presented an Islam that is that progress.'[1]

Ameer Ali (1849–1928), like Syed Ahmed, spent much of his life in government service. A barrister of Lincoln's Inn, he was the first Indian Muslim to become a High Court judge and the first Indian to be sworn a member of the British Privy Council.

In 1891 he published the *Spirit of Islam*. The first part of the book dwells on the 'sweetness of disposition, the nobility of character' of the Prophet Muhammad. In the second part Ameer Ali surveys the Prophet's teachings. 'There is a detailed and analysed apologetic for Islam on the scores of war, intolerance, women, slavery, literacy and scientific rationalism and democracy. On each it is shown, not that Islam is compatible with modern ideas

[1] Wilfred Cantwell Smith, *Modern Islam in India*, p. 49.

on these subjects, but that Islam's teaching, its spirit, is precisely those ideas.'[1]

Of women in Islam he writes:

'The Teacher who in an age when no country, no system, no community gave any right to women, maiden or married, mother or wife, who in a country where the birth of a daughter was considered a calamity, secured to the sex rights which are only unwillingly and under pressure being conceded to them by the civilized nations in the nineteenth century, deserves the gratitude of humanity. . . . Even under the laws as they stand at present in the pages of the legist, the legal position of Muslim females may be said to compare favourably with that of European women.'[2]

Of slavery:

'The whole tenor of Muhammad's teaching made "permanent chattelhood" or caste impossible; and it is simply an abuse of words to apply the word slavery, in the English sense, to any status known to Islam.'[3]

The Prophet's teaching, he maintains, was invariably progressive, democratic, humane, however much it has been misinterpreted and corrupted by successive generations.

But Ameer Ali was not satisfied with stating what Islamic society might be if the Prophet's teaching were put into practice. He went on in his brilliant *History of the Saracens* to show how Islam brought to Europe 'the splendid culture, the polished chivalry, the delicacy, grace and elegance of Arab manners which European chivalry afterwards attempted to imitate.'[4]

In the nineteenth century Islam might have much to learn from the West, but in the tenth century 'No country in the world ever enjoyed a higher degree of agricultural prosperity than Spain under the Arabs . . . the manufacture of silk and cotton was introduced by the Arabs into Spain. . . . In Granada the mere word of the citizens was considered surer than the Christian Spaniard's document.'

[1] Wilfred Cantwell Smith, *Modern Islam in India*, p. 50.
[2] Ameer Ali, *Spirit of Islam*, p. 215.
[3] *ibid.*, p. 222.
[4] Ameer Ali, *History of the Saracens*, p. 486.

The Muslim Renaissance

Ameer Ali set a style for many subsequent writers. The influence of his school has been great among the Indian Muslim middle classes. Their consciousness of the progressive nature of their religion and their pride in the historical achievements of Islam were to be powerful emotional factors in rallying them to the movement for Pakistan in the next generation.

Ameer Ali took little part in politics. One occasion in which he intervened was, however, of considerable importance. In 1909 a deputation which he led persuaded a somewhat reluctant Secretary of State, Lord Morley, to grant the Muslims separate electorates in the reforms of that year.

IQBAL. Sir Muhammad Iqbal (1873–1938) is today universally recognized in Pakistan as the great poet and prophet of the nation. There can hardly be a school or college in the country where his poems and his philosophy are not part of the prescribed curriculum, and the Pakistan Constituent Assembly has voted money for the creation of an 'Iqbal Institute' for the special study of his work.

Born of a Kashmiri family settled in the Punjab, Iqbal was educated at Lahore University, Cambridge and Munich. Before he visited Europe he was already distinguished as an Urdu lyric poet

> '*Sprung out of a dead soil*
> *Wailing like a caravan bell in the desert.*'

But it was the impact of the West which shaped his message. He was as much revolted by European civilization as he was impressed by it. He admired the energy and vigour; he loathed the ruthless competition between man and man, between nation and nation under Western capitalism.

He returned to preach that Muslims must awake, that

> '*An infidel before his idol with waking heart*
> *Is better than the religious man asleep in his mosque*';

but must awake not to go forward along the road of Western capitalism but along the distinctive Islamic path of universal

The Muslim Renaissance

brotherhood. The great period of Islam which should be studied was not the magnificent empires of Damascus, Baghdad and Spain but the simple democratic community of the first four caliphs.

'That Muslim peoples have fought and conquered like other peoples and that some of their leaders have screened their personal ambition behind the veil of religion, I do not deny; but I am absolutely sure that territorial conquest was no part of the original programme of Islam. As a matter of fact, I consider it a great loss that the progress of Islam as a conquering faith stultified the growth of those germs of an economic and democratic organization of society which I find scattered up and down the pages of the Quran and the traditions of the Prophet.'[1]

In one poem he describes the Muslims of his time as the victims of 'the Mullah, the Sultan, and the Pir' and in another writes:

> 'What is the Quran? For the capitalist a message of death
> It is the patron of the propertyless slave.'

Iqbal was a Muslim first and last, who was concerned with the transformation of Islamic society, irrespective of national boundaries, rather than with creating a nation. But his prestige was so great and his enthusiasm so boundless that he became a political leader almost in spite of himself. He was for several years a member of the Punjab Legislative Assembly, and in 1930-2 attended the Round Table Conference in London. Like Syed Ahmed, he was opposed to Muslim participation in the Indian National Congress and in favour of communal electorates and of separate communal representation in the services.

In two important speeches towards the end of his life he appeared to foresee the development of Pakistan. In 1930 in his presidential address to the Muslim League, ten years before the League adopted the programme of Pakistan, he stated:

[1] Iqbal, letter to Dr. Nicholson, 24th January 1927, published in *Dawn*, 21st April 1949.

The Muslim Renaissance

'I would like to see the Punjab, North West Frontier Province, Sind and Baluchistan amalgamated into a single state. Self government within the British Empire or without the British Empire, the formation of a consolidated North Western Indian Muslim state appears to me to be the final destiny of the Muslims, at least of North West India. . . .

'The idea need not alarm the Hindus or the British. . . . The life of Islam as a cultural force in this country very largely depends on its centralization in a specified territory.

'The Muslim demand . . . is actuated by a genuine desire for free development which is practically impossible under the type of unitary government contemplated by the nationalist Hindu politicians with a view to secure permanent communal dominance in the whole of India.

'Nor should the Hindus fear that the creation of autonomous Muslim states will mean the introduction of a kind of religious rule in such states . . .

'The principle that each group is entitled to free development on its own lines is not inspired by any feeling of narrow communalism. . . . I entertain the highest respect for the customs, laws, religious and social institutions of other communities. Nay, it is my duty according to the teaching of the Quran, even to defend their place of worship if need be.'[1]

Two years later Iqbal returned from the Round Table Conference after fruitless negotiations on the communal representation under the proposed constitutional reforms. Addressing the All India Muslim Conference, he advised the Muslims to trust neither the Hindus nor the British, but to educate and put their trust in their own people. 'The Indian Muslims should have only one political organization with provincial and district branches all over the country' . . . should 'immediately raise fifty lakhs of rupees' and 'form youth leagues and well-equipped volunteer corps throughout the country under the control and guidance of a central organization.'[2]

---

[1] *Speeches and Statements of Iqbal*, Lahore, 1944, pp 12. ff.
[2] *ibid.*, pp. 37 ff.

The Muslim Renaissance

It was this policy of 'mass contact' which Jinnah was to adopt with such success a few years later, and which converted the Muslim League from a middle class to a popular party.

Syed Ahmed, Ameer Ali and Iqbal serve to illustrate the three main trends of the Indian Muslim renaissance, the rapprochement with Western science and learning; the rediscovery of the principles of Islam and its former glory; and the impetus towards a new Islamic democracy. None of the three was a politician, but each of them was drawn into politics to emphasize the need for separate Muslim electorates. They were not, of course, alone. Aligarh's influence was extended by the educationists Chiragh Ali and Mohsin-ul-Mulk, and the poets Shibli and Hali. It became a model for Muslim colleges affiliated to the various universities of India. In Hyderabad the Osmania University, founded in 1908, made Urdu the language of instruction, and its staff greatly widened the extent of the Muslim revival by their translation work. Fifty years after Syed Ahmed's death, when Pakistan was born, though the Muslims were still behind the Hindus in education, they were able to set up a federal government, staff the services and maintain three universities with relatively little foreign help.

CHAPTER III

The Muslims and Indian Nationalism

Origin of Congress and of the League—The Bengal Partition—Mohamad Ali—The Lucknow Pact—The Khilafat Movement

While Sir Syed Ahmed was earnestly advising the Muslims of the United Provinces not to join the Indian National Congress, a distinguished Muslim, Badruddin Tyabji, was presiding over the third annual session of that body in Madras.

For the next sixty years the history of the evolution of Pakistan is inextricably linked with the history of the movement for Indian independence, and in order to understand both it is necessary to consider briefly the origin and development of the Congress, whose ranks at one time included not only the leading Indian nationalists, but many of the creators of Pakistan, including Jinnah himself.

The missionaries who came to Bengal at the beginning of the nineteenth century had both given a considerable impetus to education in the English language and had also founded a vernacular press. Macaulay in 1834 had definitely established English as the language of public instruction. Throughout the middle years of the century, therefore, more and more Indians became familiar, either in the original or in translations, with the writings of liberal political theorists such as John Stuart Mill, Tom Paine,

The Muslims and Indian Nationalism

and Mazzini, and with Western parliamentary and representative forms of government. At the same time, it was the declared policy of the British Government, which took over the direct responsibility for the administration of India from the East India Company after the Mutiny, to associate Indians increasingly in the administration. The Queen's proclamation of 1858 stated:

'It is Our ... Will that, so far as may be, Our Subjects of whatever race or creed, be freely and impartially admitted to offices in Our Service, the Duties of which they may be qualified by their education, ability and integrity duly to discharge.'

This declaration was slowly implemented. In 1861 and 1862 the Indian Councils Acts enabled non-official Indians to be nominated as members of the Legislative Councils of the Governor General and of the provincial governors. The Indian Councils Act of 1892 enabled Indian non-officials to be indirectly elected as members of those councils by municipalities and district boards. Lord Ripon created municipal and rural boards, with elected non-official majorities, in 1882. From about 1870 successful Indian candidates began to appear in the Indian Civil Service Examination.

The Indian National Congress was founded on the initiative of A. O. Hume, a British civil servant in Bengal, who hoped that it would be a vehicle of social reform. The Viceroy, Lord Dufferin, however, feeling the lack of any 'Loyal Opposition' to stimulate the Government, deliberately encouraged it to take a political character.[1] Thus from its earliest years, the Congress, after reaffirming its loyalty, would press in its annual sessions for a further extension to India of parliamentary institutions and for the further association of Indians in the administration. It had by no means a specifically Hindu character. Four of its first twenty presidents were British, and in spite of Syed Ahmed's opposition, there was usually substantial Muslim participation in the sessions.

At the beginning of the twentieth century, however, a series of events took place which both altered the character of the

[1] Sitaramayya, *History of the Indian National Congress*, Vol. I, p. 15.

The Muslims and Indian Nationalism

Congress and caused the Muslims to organize as a separate political body.

Firstly, there was a strong Hindu reaction against Western tendencies. Swami Dayanand and Swami Vivekananda asserted on the spiritual plane the superiority of Vedic Hinduism over the systems of the Western world. B. G. Tilak revived the militant Maratha political and religious tradition and, carrying it into the Congress, seemed likely to capture control from the loyal frock-coated liberals. His instincts were anti-Muslim, as well as anti-Western, and as his ideas gained ground Muslim participation in the Congress decreased. At the Benares session in 1905 the number of Muslim delegates was only seventeen out of seven hundred and fifty-six.

Tilak was assisted by the great resentment felt by the Hindu middle class towards the partition of Bengal in 1905. Curzon's object in dividing a province with a population of seventy millions was not only administrative but political. He believed that the Muslims of East Bengal were handicapped by their dependence on the Hindu city of Calcutta, and would make better progress in a separate province, governed from Dacca. Sir Bampfylde Fuller,[1] the Governor of the new province, has recorded that the administrative change was welcomed with thanksgiving prayers by the Muslims. But to the Hindus the partition was a vivisection of the Motherland, a deliberate blow at the Bengal middle class which was leading the movement for Indian self-government. Congress indeed did not countenance the terrorism and murders which now swept Bengal. But it did approve of a campaign for the boycott of British goods in an attempt to have the partition annulled.

The Muslims were impressed with the vigour of this agitation, and also by the general expectation of new political reforms which followed the return of a Liberal Government in Great Britain in 1905. They took two important steps to safeguard their interests.

Firstly, in 1906, under the leadership of the Aga Khan, they sent a deputation to the new Viceroy, Lord Minto, to express the

[1] Sir Bampfylde Fuller, *Some Personal Experiences*, p. 123.

40

need for the special protection of the Muslims if representative government were to be extended. The deputation asked for separate electorates, through which the Muslims should elect their own representatives upon municipalities, rural councils, and Provincial and Central Legislative Councils. Minto expressed his agreement with the principle, which was incorporated in the Morley-Minto reforms of 1909.[1]

Secondly, later in the same year the Nawab Viqar-al-Mulk and the Nawab of Dacca convened a meeting of leading Muslims at Dacca at which the Muslim League came into being. Its aims were specified in its first resolution as:

'(a) To promote, among the Mussalmans of India, feelings of loyalty to the British Government and to remove any misconception that may arise as to the intention of Government with regard to any of its measures.

'(b) To protect and advance the political rights and interests of the Mussalmans of India and to respectfully represent their needs and aspirations to the Government.

'(c) To prevent the rise among the Mussalmans of India of any feeling of hostility towards other communities without prejudice to the other aforementioned objects of the League.'

In 1912, under the Viceroyalty of Lord Hardinge, and on the occasion of the visit of the King-Emperor, the partition of Bengal was revoked by royal proclamation. The shock to the Muslims was tremendous. As Lord Minto told the House of Lords:

'We told the Mussalmans that the partition was a settled fact and we over and over again asserted that it must continue to be so. We assured the Mussalman population of Eastern Bengal of our appreciation of their loyalty and our determination to safeguard their interests. I should think there could have been scarcely a civil servant in India who had not declared that it

[1] What the deputation asked, and what Minto promised in this very important interview, are clearly summarized in the Simon Report, Vol. I, p. 183.

would be impossible for the British Government to reverse the decision it had come to as regards the partition of Bengal.'[1]

The Nawab of Dacca, presiding over the sixth session of the Muslim League, drew a prophetic conclusion from the episode:

'The partition gave us a great opportunity to bestir ourselves, and it awakened in our hearts the throbbings of a new national life which went pulsating through the various sections of our community in Eastern Bengal . . . We felt sure that the people of East Bengal, particularly the Muslims, would be immensely benefited by a sympathetic administration, easily accessible to them, and always ready to devote its time and attention exclusively to their welfare . . . Our ill-wishers at once perceived that the partition would necessarily bring to the fore the long-neglected claims of the Muslims of East Bengal; and although we never got more than what was justly our due, what little we gained was so much loss to them . . .

'The annulment of the partition . . . has appeared to put a premium on sedition and disloyalty, and created an impression in the minds of the irresponsible masses that even the Government can be brought down on its knees by a reckless and persistent defiance of constituted authority. Moreover, it has discredited British rule to an extent which is deeply to be regretted.'[2]

The distress of the Muslim intelligentsia at the annulment of the Bengal partition was accentuated by the encouragement which they received at this time to look westwards at the fate of their co-religionists in Turkey. Two brilliant journals in particular—Mohamed Ali's *Comrade* in Delhi and Abul Kalam Azad's *Al Hilal* in Calcutta—drew the attention of Indian Muslims to the Italo-Turkish War of 1912 and the Balkan wars which followed it; and to the apparent gradual extinction of Islamic culture in Europe and the Middle East at the hands of Western imperialism.

Maulana Mohamed Ali (1878–1930) is among the most interesting and attractive figures of the Muslim renaissance.

[1] Quoted in A. B. Rajput, *Muslim League*, p. 23.
[2] Quoted by Mohamed Ali, *Letters and Speeches*, pp. 73 ff.

The Muslims and Indian Nationalism

Educated at Aligarh and Oxford, he was assured of a distinguished career in Baroda State, but abandoned it in 1910 to write of the Muslim wrongs, founding the *Comrade*, a weekly English paper with a circulation of twenty thousand.

'Frank, blunt and outspoken, Mohamed Ali knew no diplomacy. He considered all mental reservations as villainous and outrageous offences springing from a serious flaw of character.'[1]

The two mainsprings of his life were in his own words: 'Where God commands, I am a Muslim first, a Muslim second and a Muslim last and nothing but a Muslim. But where India is concerned, I am an Indian first, an Indian second and an Indian last and nothing but an Indian.'[2]

As a Muslim, he championed the Turks against Italy and against the Balkan countries. He remained the friend of the Turks throughout the war of 1914–18, in which the Government interned him. After the war he and his brother launched the Khilafat Campaign to preserve the authority of the Sultan of Turkey as Caliph of Islam.

As an Indian Nationalist, he warmly supported Mr. Gandhi's non-co-operation movement, his boycott of British goods, and his spinning campaign. He never lost an opportunity to speak, write or go to jail for the advancement of Indian freedom, and was President of the Congress in 1924.

But at the end of his life his two guiding principles were opposed: as a Muslim, he could not agree with the Congress. A dying man, his sense of duty refused to allow him to avoid the issue. He attended the Round Table Conference in 1930 and in a remarkable letter to the Prime Minister of England, written two days before he died, made it clear that even against Gandhi he must fight for Muslim rights, and that unless the Muslim political demands were granted there would be civil war in India.[3]

[1] Afzal Iqbal in introduction to *Writings and Speeches of Mohamed Ali*, p. xii.
[2] *ibid.*, p. xiv.
[3] *ibid.*, pp. 473 ff.

The Muslims and Indian Nationalism

Maulana Abul Kalam Azad (born 1888) founded *Al Hilal*, an Urdu weekly, in Calcutta about the same time as Mohamed Ali started the *Comrade*. Abul Kalam was born in Mecca and educated in Cairo. At the age of twenty-four, his learning was prodigious, and he was already acclaimed as a 'Maulana' (religious leader). The Maulana's father had left India in disgust after the Mutiny of 1857, and the young journalist was contemptuous of the placid loyalty of the Muslims to the British. Like Mohamed Ali, Abul Kalam wrote of the wrongs suffered by the Muslims at the hands of the British in Egypt and of the British and French in Morocco. But he was more interested in internal questions and urged Indian Muslims to join with the Congress in pressing for Indian self-government. Abul Kalam never deviated from Congress. His paper was suppressed as 'pro-German', and he was interned in the 1914 war, but after his release he twice became President of the Congress and today is Minister for Education in the Indian Cabinet.

The reforms introduced in 1909, while Lord Morley was Secretary of State for India and Lord Minto was Viceroy, created elected non-official majorities for the first time in the Provincial Legislative Councils, and a non-official majority in the Viceroy's Legislative Council. For the first time also the principle of direct election from constituencies was recognized, though the franchise was very limited. Lord Minto kept his promise to the Muslims, who were given separate electorates. The Councils were essentially advisory, with no control over the executive, and the result was to increase the demand for self-government rather than to diminish it. In 1913 the Muslim League formally adopted the objective already accepted by Congress—Indian self-government within the Empire, though it stipulated that the system of government must be of a form 'suitable to India'.

The outbreak of war in 1914 and the tremendous losses suffered by the Allied forces put a premium on India's loyalty and India's armed forces. Mohamed Ali proudly refused to exploit the British difficulties: 'Concessions are asked for and accepted in peace. We are not Russian Poles. We need no bribes.'[1] Gandhi recruited troops for the army. But both among Muslims and Hindus there was a hope that India's loyalty would be rewarded spontaneously by further steps to self-government. Strong personalities on both sides worked for Hindu-Muslim unity, making joint demands for further reforms. Largely owing to the efforts of Mohammed Ali Jinnah, a rising Bombay barrister, the League agreed to hold its annual conferences at the same time and place as the Congress, and at the end of 1916 Congress and League signed the famous 'Lucknow Pact'. For the first and only time there was agreement between these parties on the future Constitution of India. The Muslims were to have one-third of the Indian elective seats in the All India Legislature. In the Provinces they were to have 50 per cent of the Indian elective seats in the Punjab; 30 per cent in the United Provinces; 40 per cent in Bengal; 25 per cent in Bihar; 15 per cent in the Central Provinces; 15 per cent in Madras and 33.3 per cent in Bombay. Both in the Provinces and at the Centre the Muslims were to have their own separate electorates. No bill affecting a particular community should be proceeded with in any council if three-fourths of the representatives of that community opposed it.

In August 1917 the Secretary of State for India, Edwin Montagu, made a declaration in the House of Commons which aroused high hopes in Indian Nationalist circles.

'The policy of His Majesty's Government, with which the Government of India are in complete accord, is that of the increasing association of Indians in every branch of the administration, and the gradual development of self-governing institutions with a view to the progressive realization of responsible government in India as an integral part of the British Empire.'

Montagu shortly afterwards made a lengthy visit to India and as a result a further step towards Indian self-government was granted. The Montagu-Chelmsford Reforms of 1919, however,

[1] Rajput, *Muslim League*, p. 28.

conceded far less than the Lucknow Pact had demanded. The powers, franchise and membership of the Provincial Legislative Councils were enlarged, and certain 'transferred' subjects, such as Health and Education, were entrusted to Indian ministers responsible to the Councils. But Law and Order and Finance, 'reserved subjects', remained the responsibility of the provincial governors and of their nominated councillors. Similarly at the Centre, though two chambers now replaced the previous Legislative Council and though elected members were to be in a majority in each, the Governor General retained the right to 'certify' any legislation which he considered essential, and his Executive Council was responsible not to the Legislature but to the Secretary of State in London.

Such concessions were quite unacceptable to the majority of the Congress and of the League. Disappointment with the reforms, resentment at the strong measures which the Government took to put down certain anarchical disorders, and bitterness over the Amritsar massacres led to a decision of the Congress to boycott the legislatures and launch a nation-wide non-co-operation movement, under Mr. Gandhi's leadership, to bring the Government to its knees.

Meanwhile, Muslim interest in politics was less in internal reforms than in the fate of Turkey under the peace treaties of 1919. The intense interest of Indian Muslims in Turkey had been summed up years earlier by Syed Ahmed.

'When there were many Muslim kingdoms we did not feel so much grief when one of them was destroyed; now that so few are left we feel the loss even of a small one. If Turkey is conquered that will be a great grief, for she is the last of the great powers left to Islam. We are afraid that we shall become like the Jews, a people without a country of our own.'[1]

Foremost in drawing the attention of the Muslims to the danger to Turkey in the peace settlement was Mohamed Ali. Indian Muslims had remained loyal even when Britain and India were at war with Turkey. Lloyd George, informed of Indian Muslim

[1] Statement to Sir Theodore Morison, quoted in *Political India*, p. 95.

The Muslims and Indian Nationalism

opinion, had clearly stated in January 1918 that the Allies would not deprive Turkey of her capital or lands in Asia Minor and Thrace. Yet at the end of the war the Greek armies were launched against Turkey, as it seemed, in a campaign of extermination. The Holy Places which the Prophet had bidden Muslims to preserve were to be placed under non-Muslim mandates. The Sultan of Turkey, Commander of the Faithful, the Successor and Khalifa (Caliph) of the Prophet, was to be deprived of the bulk of his territory. Mohamed Ali went in person to London and Paris to protest, and only when he was politely ignored, returned to India to preach that the Government of India, as a party to the peace treaties, had trampled the law of Islam underfoot and was an infidel government, no longer to be obeyed. Under his influence thousands of Muslims in Sind and the Frontier shook the hated dust of India from their feet and migrated to Afghanistan, where they were turned back, many to perish on the road home.

The impulsiveness of Mohamed Ali, and the political astuteness of Gandhi, thus brought about a strange alliance against the British. Mohamed Ali saw in Gandhi 'A visionary who is at the same time a thoroughly practical person, the most large-hearted man in the world today, and one who is also among the topmost men of the world in intellectual greatness.'[1] He joined with Gandhi in the latter's non-violent non-co-operation movement. Everything British was to be avoided; taxes were to be unpaid; workers to strike; shopkeepers to refuse to sell British goods; students to leave British colleges; until the two very different objects were attained—the restoration of the Caliph's authority and the granting of Home Rule.

For the Muslims the campaign ended in complete failure. The Turks themselves, under Mustafa Kamal, abolished the Caliphate and exiled the Caliph in 1922. The non-co-operation movement led to widespread and irresponsible violence. The Muslim Moplahs rose in Madras to create a 'Caliphate state' and slaughtered not only a few British officials but far more of

[1] Rajput, *Muslim League*, p. 31.

The Muslims and Indian Nationalism

their Hindu neighbours. Finally, when a mob burned some police constables alive at Chauri Chaura, Gandhi called off the movement. The people, he said, were not yet ready for the way of non-violence. The Muslims, who had never been intellectually convinced of the effectiveness of non-violence, were left baffled and frustrated. The years that followed were full of bitter and pointless communal riots between Hindu and Muslim peasants and artisans, and there was an increasing struggle between Hindu and Muslim middle classes for jobs in the Indianized services and power under the new reforms. Never again was the spirit of unity of the Lucknow Pact and the non-co-operation movement recaptured.

CHAPTER IV

The Muslims as a Nation

*Communal Riots—The Reforms—Elections of 1937—
The League as a Popular Party—The Lahore Resolution
—Influence of Jinnah*

D r. Ambedkar, in a careful analysis of communal disturbances between 1920 and 1940, has described the period as one of 'civil war between Hindus and Muslims, interrupted by brief intervals of armed peace'.[1] In Cawnpore in March 1931 he estimates that between 400 and 500 persons were killed; in Bombay Province between February 1929 and April 1938 there were 210 days of rioting, causing 560 deaths and 4,500 injuries. In Bengal he calculates that between 1922 and 1927 35,000 women were abducted, and he gives details of public rapes, assassinations, and burning alive which would be startling if the atrocities of 1947 had not dwarfed these.

The immediate causes of the disturbances were petty. The Muslim procession of mourning at Mohurram clashed with a Hindu festival; Hindu temple bells or wedding processions disturbed Muslim prayers in a mosque; the Muslim sacrifice of a cow at the Bakr-Id festival irritated Hindu sentiment. Or, among the middle classes, publication of pamphlets or articles attacking religion led to resentment, and even murder.

There was, however, a permanent economic friction which enhanced the communal friction.[2] In East Bengal most landlords

---

[1] Ambedkar, *Pakistan*, pp. 152 ff. Dr. Ambedkar, leader of the Scheduled Castes or 'Untouchables' is now Law Minister in the Indian Cabinet.

[2] Pandit Nehru, the present Prime Minister of India, gives great weight to this factor. See Nehru, *Autobiography*, chapter 56; also p. 138.

The Muslims as a Nation

were Hindus, whilst the cultivators were Muslims. In the Punjab the bankers and richer merchants were Hindus and the majority of their debtors Muslims. Throughout India the new educated Muslim middle class was striving to obtain appointments both in government service and in commerce which had hitherto been held by Hindus for lack of Muslim competition. There were two particular reasons which may explain the intensity of communal riots in the 'twenties. Firstly, as was noted by Mrs. Besant, Pandit Nehru,[1] and other contemporary observers, the non-co-operation movement of 1919–22 had caused a general lessening of respect of established authority which continued to be manifest after the movement ceased. Secondly, as the Simon Commission noted, the communal riots were 'a manifestation of the anxieties and ambitions aroused in both the communities by the prospect of India's political future. So long as authority was firmly established in British hands and self-government was not thought of, Hindu-Muslim rivalry was confined within a narrow field . . . The coming of the Reforms and the anticipation of what may follow have given new point to Hindu-Muslim competition. The one community naturally lays claim to the rights of a majority, and relies upon its greater qualifications of better education and greater wealth; the other is all the more determined on those accounts to secure effective protection for its members, and does not forget that it represents the previous conquerors of the country.'[2]

After the collapse of the Khilafat movement and the end of non-co-operation, there was disagreement on policy both in the Congress and among Muslim political leaders. Although the Congress as a whole refused to participate in the new Legislative Councils created by the 1919 reforms, a Swaraj Party, led by C. R. Das and Motilal Nehru, fought elections and took up their seats with the avowed purpose of wrecking the constitution from within. Among the Muslims, Mohamed Ali and Abul

[1] Nehru, *Autobiography* p. 86.
[2] Simon Report, vol. i, p. 29.

The Muslims as a Nation

Kalam Azad continued with the Congress. Jinnah led an independent party, consisting mainly of Muslims, in the Central Legislative Assembly.

In a series of All Party Conferences and Unity Conferences, sincere attempts were made to check the communal riots and to draft an agreed Constitution for a free India. But the heightened communal feeling was reflected in the divergence of leaders of all communities from the terms of the Lucknow Pact of 1916. The Muslim claim to separate electorates was followed by similar claims of the Sikhs and Hindu depressed classes; and the Hindu Mahasabha was founded to safeguard the majority rights of the Hindus. Thus, on the one hand, when a draft Constitution was produced by an All Party Committee, chaired by Motilal Nehru, in 1929, it was unable to accept the Muslim claim to one-third of the seats in the Central Legislature, which had been granted in the Lucknow Pact. On the other hand, the Muslim League in its Fourteen Points, put forward the same year, made additional demands. Whereas in the Lucknow Pact the residuary powers in the Federal Constitution were to lie with the Centre, the resolution of 1929 required them to be left with the provinces. And whereas the Lucknow Pact underweighted the Muslim representation in the provinces where they were in a majority (Punjab 50 per cent; Bengal 40 per cent), the 1929 resolution demanded that Muslim majorities in those provinces should be permanently assured, and that two new Muslim-majority provinces, Sind and North West Frontier Province, should be created.

In 1916, Indian self-government had seemed a remote ideal. But by 1929 the British Government had made a substantial step towards it in the Montagu-Chelmsford Reforms and was preparing another. All communities had thus had ample opportunity to reflect on their probable position in a free India. In 1916 the Muslims had been mainly concerned with the protection of their position under elected provincial governments in provinces where they were in a minority. By 1929 they were far more concerned with their position as a permanent minority under a federal All India Government. Their best safeguard seemed to be to maintain their majority provinces in the north-west and east of India as bastions of Muslim influence, and to limit severely the authority of the proposed federal government. Their representatives at the Round Table Conference, called by the British Government in 1930–2 to consider further reforms, urged this policy. In this there was fundamental agreement between Muslims as diverse as the Aga Khan, Jinnah and Mohamed Ali.

The 1935 Government of India Act by no means satisfied either Congress or the Muslims. True, 'dyarchy' was abolished in the provinces, where ministers, holding all the portfolios, now became responsible to elected Legislative Assemblies: there was provision for a responsible federal government at the Centre when a sufficient number of the princely states acceded to the Federation: and the franchise was widened to include in the provinces thirty million voters out of the total population of two hundred and ninety-five millions in British India. But Congress resented the 'safeguards' for such matters as preservation of peace and tranquillity and protection of minorities, which were left in the hands of provincial governors, and was opposed to accepting the autocratic princes at the Centre as representatives of their peoples. The Muslim League found certain of its demands granted. Sind and the North West Frontier Province were created as new self-governing Muslim-majority provinces. But in the Punjab, where the Muslims received 49 per cent of the seats, and in Bengal, where they received 47 per cent, their majority in the Provincial Assemblies was not assured.[1] Jinnah in the Central Assembly described the scheme for provincial governments as 'unsatisfactory' and the scheme for the Central Government as 'fundamentally bad'.

In fact the federal part of the 1935 Act was never implemented, but both Congress and League contested the elections for the new Provincial Assemblies in 1937. Congress, brilliantly led by Jawarharlal Nehru, with a programme of economic and social

[1] The Reforms of 1909, 1919 and 1935, and their consequences, have been clearly summarized in Coupland, *India: A Restatement*, pp. 103–16, 142–8.

reform, obtained outright majorities in five out of the eleven Provincial Assemblies, and was the largest party in two others. Congress ministries were formed in Bombay, Madras, Central Provinces, United Provinces, Bihar, Orissa, and the North West Frontier Province. The Muslim League did less well. In 1937 it was still a middle-class organization which had made little effort to obtain a mass following. Nor was it in opposition to the Congress's social programme. Jinnah, as chairman of the League's Election Board, made it clear that co-operation with the Congress was desired, provided that it was a genuine coalition between independent parties.

'There is really no substantial difference now at any rate between the League and the Congress . . . I have often said that I am trying to see that Muslims should wholeheartedly and sincerely adhere to the policy and programme of the All India Muslim League, which is both national and patriotic, and we shall always be glad to co-operate with the Congress in their constructive programme.' But 'It is no use encouraging individual Muslims to come into the fold of the Congress in their constructive programme.'[1]

In Bengal and the Punjab coalition governments were formed under the leadership of Muslims who were members neither of Congress nor the League. In the North West Frontier, Dr. Khan Sahib's Muslim Nationalists allied themselves with the Congress. But in the Hindu-majority provinces where the League captured a substantial number of the Muslim seats, it confidently expected to be asked to form coalition ministries with the Congress. This was particularly true of the United Provinces, where the League's candidates had run on a common platform with the Congress, had won more Muslim seats than any other party, and had received what it considered to be definite assurances of a coalition before the elections. When the results were declared and Congress found itself with an overall majority, however, it offered the League terms which no independent political party could have accepted. Leaguers would be taken into the Cabinet only if

[1] Saiyid, *Jinnah*, p. 559.

53

the League dissolved its parliamentary organization and if all its representatives became members of the Congress. Thereafter all policy decisions must be made by majority vote of the Congress Party.[1]

The Congress's procedure after the 1937 elections could be justified constitutionally and by normal parliamentary standards. The Constitution was respected by taking individual Muslims or Muslim Congressmen into each of their ministries. And in parliamentary practice no party with an overall majority is obliged to form a coalition with a smaller party. The League view, however, was that as the Muslim ministers were being appointed not on account of their personal claims but as representatives of the Muslims, they should command the confidence of the majority of the Muslim members of the Legislature. They pointed to the precedent of the Punjab, where the Muslim Premier, Sir Sikander Hayat Khan, in spite of having an overwhelming majority in the house, invited the leader of the Hindu Mahasabha to nominate one minister. No single event did more than this to bring Pakistan into being. Men such as Khaliquzzaman, the League leader in the United Provinces, who had combined membership of the League with membership of the Congress for twenty-five years, found themselves bound to choose between the two. They felt betrayed and indignant; and, in vigilant opposition, took every opportunity to make public the wrongs, real or trivial, suffered by Muslims under Congress rule. The League set up an All India Committee, presided over by the Raja of Pirpur, to investigate the 'hardship, ill-treatment and injustice that is meted out to the Muslims in various Congress Government provinces'. Its report, perhaps, does not now seem very shocking by comparison with the events of 1947. It states that the Congress flag has been hoisted on government buildings; that Muslim children have been made to sing the Bande Mataram and worship the portrait of Mr. Gandhi; that Muslims have been intimidated from eating

[1] The ruling of the President of the Congress on the terms on which Muslim Leaguers could be taken into the United Provinces Ministry is quoted by Coupland, *India: A Restatement*, appendix 3.

beef and excluded from local bodies; that the Urdu language and script have been discouraged; that the police have favoured Hindus in communal riots, and that Hindus have received preference in the Services.

But it was just such irritations and the exploitation of them which for the first time obtained for the Muslim League the overwhelming support of the Muslim lower-middle and working classes. Jinnah reduced the annual membership fee of the League to two annas,[1] and, urged by Iqbal,[2] conducted a fiery campaign in the country, proclaiming that Islam was in danger. At Lucknow he declared : 'On the very threshold of what little power and responsibility is given, the majority community have clearly shown their hand, that Hindustan is for the Hindus. Only the Congress masquerades under the name of nationalism.' At Karachi he accused the average Congressman 'of behaving and acting towards the Mussalmans in a much worse manner than the British did towards Indians'. At Patna 'The Congress has now killed every hope of Hindu Muslim settlement in the right royal fashion of Fascism'.

Between 1938 and the end of 1942 the League won forty-six out of fifty-six by-elections in the Muslim constituencies throughout the provinces.[3] The Premiers of the Punjab and Bengal joined the League, bringing most of their followers with them. When the Congress ministries resigned in October 1939, as a protest at the Viceroy's declaration of war without consulting the Assemblies, Jinnah declared a 'day of deliverance and thanksgiving, as a mark of relief that the Congress regime has at last ceased to function'. This was enthusiastically celebrated by Muslims throughout the country.

The indignation felt by Muslims at what they had experienced under, or what they had heard of, the Congress provincial governments caused them once more to reflect on what their position would be under an All India federation in which they

[1] Two pence or three cents.
[2] Saiyid, *Jinnah*, pp. 564 ff.
[3] Coupland, *Indian Politics*, part ii, appendix vi.

The Muslims as a Nation

appeared likely, in spite of all safeguards, to be a permanent minority under a Congress government. In August 1939 the League urged the British Government to abandon finally the federal part of the 1935 Constitution. Six months later, at its annual session at Lahore, it went further and, in the most famous and important resolution in its history, unanimously resolved that:

'No constitutional plan would be workable in this country or acceptable to the Muslims unless it is designed on the following basic principles, viz., that geographically contiguous units are demarcated into regions which should be so constituted with such territorial adjustments as may be necessary, that the areas in which the Muslims are numerically in a majority, as in the north-western and eastern zones of India, should be grouped to constitute "Independent States" in which the constituent units shall be autonomous and sovereign.'

The Indian Press immediately grasped the significance of this decision and called it the 'Pakistan resolution', taking the name from the writings of Choudhury Rehmat Ali of Cambridge.[1] Henceforth the League was firmly pledged to the establishment of an autonomous Muslim state. It remained for it to prove that in this it represented the overwhelming majority of Indian Muslims; and having done so, to attain its objective despite the hostility of almost all non-Muslim Indians and the incredulity of most Englishmen.

No one had played a greater part in persuading the League to adopt the 'Pakistan Resolution' than Jinnah. 'The Hindus and Muslims', he said in his presidential speech at Lahore, 'belong to two different religious philosophies, social customs, literatures. They neither intermarry nor interdine, and indeed they.

---

[1] 'Pakistan is both a Persian and Urdu word. It is composed of letters taken from the names of all our homelands—"Indian" and "Asian". That is, Panjab, Afghania (North West Frontier Province), Kashmir, Iran, Sindh (including Kutch and Kathiawar), Tukharistan, Afghanistan and Balochistan. It means the land of the Paks—the spiritually pure and clean. It symbolizes the religious beliefs and ethnical stocks of our people; and it stands for all the territorial constituents of our original Fatherland.'—Rehmat Ali, *Pakistan*, p. 225.

belong to two different civilizations which are based on con-
flicting ideas and conceptions . . . To yoke together two such
nations under a single state, one as a numerical minority, and
the other as a majority, must lead to growing discontent and
final destruction of any fabric that may be so built up for the
government of such a state.[1]' Yet this was the same Jinnah who
as architect of the Lucknow Pact in 1916 had been hailed by
Hindus as the 'Ambassador of Unity'. It is interesting to trace
the change in his position, for in it the great majority of politically conscious Muslims followed or accompanied him.

Mohammed Ali Jinnah (1876–1948) was born in Karachi of
a wealthy merchant family. At the age of sixteen he went to
England, where he qualified as a barrister of Lincoln's Inn. On
his return he earned an immediate reputation and lucrative
practice at the Bombay bar, and, turning naturally to politics,
served his apprenticeship with moderate Congressmen, Naoroji
and Gokhale. In 1909 he was elected by the Muslims of Bombay
as their representative on the Governor General's Legislative
Council, where he attracted considerable notice and was the
first member to pilot through a private member's bill. Already a
well-known Congressman, pledged to Indian independence, in
1913 he also became a member of the Muslim League, of which
he was President at the time of the Lucknow Pact of 1916. His
presidential speech on that occasion has much interest in view of
his subsequent career and of the bitter allegations of inconsis-
tency which have been made against him by Indian Nationalists.
Emphatically stressing the need for separate Muslim electorates,
he said:

'I have been a staunch Congressman throughout my public
life and have been no lover of sectarian cries, but it appears to
me that the reproach of "separatism" sometimes levelled at
Mussalmans is singularly inept and wide of the mark, when I see
this great communal organization rapidly growing into a powerful factor for the birth of a United India. A minority must, above
everything else, have a complete sense of security before its

[1] Jinnah, *Speeches and Writings*, vol. i, p. 153.

broader political sense can be evoked for co-operation and united endeavour in the national tasks. To the Mussalmans of India that security can only come through adequate and effective safeguards as regards their political existence as a community.'[1]

Jinnah strongly opposed the non-co-operation movement of 1919–22. At the Nagpur Conference of the Congress in 1920, out of 14,582 delegates, of whom 1,050 were Muslims, he was the only dissentient to the resolution which launched the movement. He subsequently wrote to Gandhi: 'Your methods have already caused split and division in almost every institution that you have approached hitherto . . . and your extreme programme has for the moment struck the imagination mostly of the inexperienced youth and the ignorant and illiterate. All this means disorganization and chaos.'[2] He deplored the appeals which were made to students to come out of government-aided schools and colleges, and whilst agreeing that the political reforms of 1919 were inadequate, believed that the new Constitution ought to be worked. He continued, therefore, as a member of the Central Legislative Assembly, leading an independent Muslim party, and becoming perhaps the most skilful parliamentarian of the time.

After the collapse of the Khilafat movement, he revived the Muslim League and was largely responsible for drafting its Fourteen Points in 1929. When the Round Table Conference ended, weary of fruitless inter-communal conferences, he remained in England to practise law, only returning in 1934 to shape the Muslim League's attitude towards the new Constitution. Had he died in 1937 he would be mainly remembered as an eminent Indian Nationalist and parliamentarian in the tradition of Naoroji and Gokhale. Indeed his memory even now lives on as such in Bombay, where the present Congress headquarters, 'Jinnah Hall', was erected in his honour after his spectacular opposition to Lord Willingdon in 1918.

But between 1937 and 1940 there occurred a remarkable change. For not only did Jinnah reverse his whole life's work

[1] Saiyid, *Jinnah*, p. 876. [2] *ibid*., p. 265.

of Hindu-Muslim unity, but for the first time, at the age of sixty, he became a popular figure, 'the Quaid-i-Azam'—'Great Leader'. Undoubtedly he was partly influenced by Iqbal, who was in constant correspondence with him and wrote:

'I have no doubt that you fully realize the gravity of the situation as far as Muslim India is concerned. The League will have to finally decide whether it will remain a body representing the upper classes of Indian Muslims or the Muslim masses, who have so far, with good reason, taken no interest in it.'[1]

Money meant nothing to Jinnah. He commanded the highest fees at the Bombay bar. Office meant little. He never accepted an official position until he became the first Governor General of Pakistan. His bitterest enemies cannot now successfully maintain that his conversion was not genuine, and he was accompanied in it by lifelong Congressmen such as Khaliquzzaman, by honest aristocrats such as Nazimuddin, and shrewd politicians such as Fazl Huq.

What occurred between 1937 and 1940 was not the evolution of a new political theory. One of the founders of the Hindu Mahasabha, Lala Lajput Rai, had suggested the partition of India between Hindus and Muslims as early as 1924. Savarkar, the President of the Mahasabha, had frequently referred to the Hindus and Muslims as 'two nations'. Iqbal had placed the idea of a Muslim state before the League in 1930. Rehmat Ali had invented the name of Pakistan in 1933 and campaigned indefatigably for its creation ever since. But before 1937 the majority of the Muslim middle class would probably have agreed with the representatives of the League and the Muslim Conference, who told the Joint Select Committee of the British Parliament in 1933 that Pakistan was 'only a student's scheme . . . chimerical and impracticable'.[2]

As for the villager, the cultivator and the artisan, who formed 90 per cent of India's population, he lived in 1937 much as he

[1] Saiyid, *Jinnah*, p. 564.
[2] Report of Joint Select Committee on Indian Reforms: Minutes of Evidence, questions 9,598 to 9,600.

had lived for a hundred years. Hindu and Muslim dwelt in the same village, but in different parts of it. The Muslim did not eat with the Hindu or marry into his family. His food, his dress, his name, and often his profession, were distinctly Muslim, and when he died he was buried, whereas the Hindu was burned. Politics played little part in his life. For the franchise was limited, and ever since he could remember, whatever politicians might say, the British dispensed justice, maintained law and order and collected taxes. But in 1937 Congress ministers in homespun dress sat in the Secretariat and controlled the British revenue officials, magistrates and police officers. The Congress flag with its spinning wheel flew on government buildings. And however hard Congress leaders tried to make it otherwise, the Congress was an overwhelmingly Hindu organization. When, therefore, he was told by League organizers of the wrongs which his Muslim brethren were suffering under Congress Raj, he believed them. The suggestion of Hindu domination was intolerable. Once he had heard that Islam was in danger he clung to that idea, and no talk of communal weightages and safeguards could move him: Congress's admirable economic and social reforms seemed irrelevant. If the British were leaving there must either be Hindu rule or Muslim rule. Islam was in danger, and the only leader he would follow was one who claimed to save it. True enough, it was the Muslim League leaders, excluded from power and indignant, who had first raised the cry, but once it was raised nothing could silence it.

'No power on earth can prevent Pakistan', said Jinnah in 1940. He spoke shrewdly. For, as we can see now from the elections of 1946, the whole League leadership could not have checked the impetus to Pakistan even had it wished. The historical importance of the period of the Congress ministries lies not so much in the question of whether the Muslim grievances were great or whether they were exaggerated, but in the fact that the overwhelming majority of Muslims believed them to exist. What is significant is not whether racially, or by any anthropological test, the Muslims were a nation, but that the overwhelming majority of Indian Muslims felt themselves to be Muslims first and Indians only second. No Indian Nationalist can forgive Jinnah for what seemed to be the abandonment of the principles of a lifetime. But the Pakistanis will always venerate his memory because at a critical moment in history he came out of the rarefied atmosphere of the council chamber and the conference room to give vehement expression to a people's inarticulate desire to form a distinct and independent political unit.

CHAPTER V

The Birth of Pakistan

The Second World War—Attitude of Congress and League—The Cripps Mission—Gandhi and Jinnah—The Cabinet Mission—The Mountbatten Plan—The Final Settlement

The somewhat vague terms of the Lahore resolution of 1940 were clarified shortly afterwards by Jinnah in an interview which he gave to the Associated Press of America.[1] Pakistan was to be a democratic federal state comprising the existing provinces of the North West Frontier, Baluchistan, Sind and the Punjab in the west; and Bengal and Assam in the east. The League's claim to represent the majority of Indian Muslims in putting forward this objective was ridiculed by the Congress, to whom the creation of a sovereign state on the basis of a common religion seemed a historical anachronism; and its inclusion of two separate portions of the Indian subcontinent, separated by a thousand miles, seemed a geographical absurdity. Jinnah, to whom great tactical authority was delegated by his Working Committee, was far less concerned to enter into arguments on the merits or nature of Pakistan than to consolidate the League membership and maintain its enthusiasm for the idea of Pakistan, until fresh elections to the Assemblies should prove its strength. He was in no hurry to press for the independence of India from Britain until he was sure of the simultaneous independence of Pakistan from India.

[1] Quoted in Rajput, *Muslim League*, p. 75.

The Birth of Pakistan

The attitudes of Congress and of the League to the British Government during the world war of 1939–45 were therefore very different. The Congress provincial ministries in Madras, Central Provinces, Bihar, United Provinces, Bombay, Orissa, and North West Frontier Province resigned in October 1939, after passing through their Assemblies identical resolutions deploring the declaration of war 'without the consent of the Indian people' and calling for the immediate treatment of India as 'an independent nation entitled to frame her own constitution'. As the war continued the Congress demand for immediate independence became more urgent. In October 1940 Gandhi launched an individual civil-disobedience campaign, in which Congressmen were nominated by him to make speeches opposing India's participation in the war and courting imprisonment. In the course of this, national leaders such as Patel and Nehru, together with most of the former Congress privincial ministers, were arrested. There was a general jail delivery in 1941; but after the failure of Sir Stafford Cripps' Mission in 1942, Congress went into 'open rebellion', sanctioning 'a mass struggle on non-violent lines on the widest possible scale' against 'an imperialist and authoritarian Government'.[1] As a result, the Congress Working Committee remained in jail from August 1942 until June 1945 and Gandhi himself was detained between August 1942 and May 1944.

The League attitude towards the Government throughout the war was one of limited co-operation. A Working Committee resolution in September 1939 expressed deep sympathy for Poland, England and France, but asked that Indian Muslim troops should on no account be used to fight against Muslims, demanded fair treatment for the Arabs in Palestine, called for justice for Muslims in Congress-ruled provinces, and for the abandonment of the federal part of the 1935 Constitution. On all these points they received a measure of satisfaction, and although the League itself refused to support the war effort unless the

[1] Bombay Resolution of All India Congress Committee, 8th August, 1942.

Government firmly committed itself in favour of Pakistan, its provincial ministries gave quiet assistance.

The League gained by the absence of Congress from the political scene. At one time or another there were League ministries in Bengal, the Punjab, Sind, the North West Frontier and Assam. In the remaining provinces, the Assemblies were prorogued and the administration carried on by British Governors with official advisers. Jinnah, regularly re-elected as President of the League, strongly asserted party discipline. When the Viceroy appointed the Muslim provincial Premiers as members of his National Defence Council in 1941, Jinnah obtained their immediate resignations because the invitations had not come through party channels. By doing so, he lost the allegiance of Fazl Huq, Premier of Bengal, but in the event the League was strengthened, for Fazl Huq was replaced by the loyal Leaguer, Nazimuddin. Similarly, although in the Punjab Khizr Hayat Khan successfully defied Jinnah and remained Premier of a coalition government, on his expulsion from the League he lost the support of the great part of the Muslim electorate.

The British policy throughout the war was that, for its duration, defence and the general responsibility for the Central Government must remain with the Viceroy, who would, however, welcome representatives of the major parties as members of his executive council. At the same time, it was hoped that agreement would be reached by those parties for an advance to Dominion status after the war. In April 1942 Sir Stafford Cripps visited India with specific British proposals both for the interim government and the postwar constitution, which he discussed with Congress and League representatives. For the first time, the right of individual provinces to stay out of the proposed Indian Union, and even to form a separate federation, was acknowledged. Congress rejected the proposals because they did not give adequate immediate responsibility and because they were 'a severe blow to the conception of Indian Unity'.[1] The Muslim League rejected them because they did not explicitly create

[1] Congress Resolution of 2nd April 1942.

64

Pakistan. Many observers[1] believed, however, that the League would have accepted the proposals had the Congress done so.

One courageous and eminently rational Congressman tried to break the deadlock. Rajagopalachari, a former President of the Congress and Premier of Madras, was appalled by India's continual dissensions and lack of a popular government while the Japanese armies and fleet were at her door. He moved two resolutions in the All India Congress Committee in May 1942, the first conceding the principle of Pakistan and the second in favour of forming a Congress-League coalition in Madras. He was heavily defeated, and the Committee resolved instead that 'any proposal to disintegrate India by giving liberty to any state or territorial unit to secede from the Indian Union or Federation would be highly detrimental to the best interests of the people of the different states and provinces and the country as a whole, and the Congress cannot agree to any such proposal'. Undaunted, Rajagopalachari resigned from the Congress, and when Gandhi was released from jail in 1944 persuaded him to discuss with Jinnah a formula entitled 'basis for settlement between the Indian National Congress and the All India Muslim League'. Its essence was that the League should co-operate with the Congress in an interim government, and that after the termination of the war a plebiscite should be held in Muslim majority areas, which should be allowed to form an autonomous state if they so wished.

The Gandhi-Jinnah talks of September 1944, however, were unsuccessful. Gandhi could not accept the thesis that the Muslims were a nation. He confessed that 'As I imagine the Lahore resolution in practice, I see nothing but ruin for the whole of India'. India's independence must first be obtained, he argued, then, even if Muslim majority areas wished to constitute a separate state, there must be common arrangements for defence, commerce, communications, foreign affairs and customs. Jinnah regarded Gandhi's attitude as a negation of Pakistan, and in any case questioned his capacity to negotiate on behalf of the Congress.

[1] Such as Sir Reginald Coupland, *The Cripps Mission*, p. 36.

The Birth of Pakistan

There could hardly be a more striking contrast than these two unquestioned leaders of the greatest political parties in India at one of the most critical moments in her history. Jinnah, in immaculate European dress, lived in a mansion on Malabar Hill. He regarded politics as an occupation for professionals, could be seen only by appointment, and made public statements occasionally and very carefully. Gandhi wore a single piece of homespun cloth and lived in a hut in a remote village in Central India. He was accessible to anyone who took the trouble to come and see him and was prepared to advise and pronounce on almost any political, social or moral problem which was brought to him. When Gandhi and Jinnah met or corresponded, there appeared to be an almost complete lack of mutual understanding, and the training which each had received as barrister of a London Inn only served to sharpen their differences. To Jinnah, the parliamentarian, Gandhi's introduction into politics of such elements as cow protection, spinning and 'satygraha' was repugnant and irrelevant. He left the Congress when Gandhi became its acknowledged leader and his subsequent comments on Gandhi's leadership were often derisive.[1] It was against Gandhi's principles to utter personal disparagement of Jinnah, or indeed of anyone else. But the embittered view of his colleagues is reflected in a description of Gandhi and Jinnah in 1944 by the official historian and present President of the Congress.

'Look at that picture and this, Gandhi the embodiment of patience and faith, meekness and humility, truth and non-violence; Jinnah the very incarnation of conceit and self-consciousness, of dictatorial temper and diplomacy and strategy...'[2]

After the end of three weeks of conversations, Gandhi's verdict was that 'Mr. Jinnah is sincere, but I think he is suffering from hallucination when he imagines that an unnatural division of India could bring either happiness or prosperity to the people concerned'.[3] Jinnah observed: 'Here is an apostle and a devotee

[1] One of the most sustained examples is in his address to the Muslim League at Delhi in 1943. Jinnah, *Speeches and Writings*, vol. i, pp. 458 ff.
[2] P. Sitaramayya, *History of the Congress*, vol. ii, p. 598.
[3] M. K. Gandhi, *To the Protagonists of Pakistan*, p. 155.

of non-violence threatening us with a fight to the knife ... For an ordinary mortal like me there is no room in the presence of his "inner voice".[1]

After the defeat of Germany in the spring of 1945, the Congress Working Committee was released. The Viceroy, Lord Wavell, called a conference of political leaders at Simla, proposed to them that his Executive Council should immediately be completely Indianized, except for the Viceroy and the Commander-in-Chief, and asked each party to nominate representatives to it. The Council was to function as an 'Interim Government' until the Japanese War was over and until agreement was reached on the ultimate constitution. The immediate cause of the failure of this proposal was Jinnah's insistence that only the League should have the right to nominate the Muslim members of the Council. This claim was not acceptable either to the Congress, which wished to have the right to nominate a Congress Muslim, or to the Viceroy, who wished the Punjab Unionist Party to be represented on his Council by a Muslim.

Shortly after the failure of the Simla Conference, the Labour Party came into power in England, and the Japanese War ended. One of the first actions of the Labour Government was to order elections both for the Central and Provincial Assemblies, which had been postponed during the war. At the same time, it was announced that it was the intention of His Majesty's Government to convene as soon as possible after the elections a Constitution-making body for British India. Simultaneously, discussions would be held with the Indian states of their place in the new Constitution.

The elections were a triumphant vindication of Jinnah's claim to represent the Muslims. The League captured all the Muslim seats in the Central Assembly, and in the Provincial Assemblies won 446 out of a total of 495 Muslim seats, its only failure being in the North West Frontier Province. Congress had a similar victory in the General (non-Muslim) constituencies. The stage was now set for a settlement. The British Government was

[1] Jinnah, *Speeches and Writings*, vol. ii, p. 215.

pledged to grant Indian independence. Congress and League had proved their strength as the successors to the British authority.

In March 1946 the British Cabinet sent out three of its members—Lord Pethick-Lawrence, Sir Stafford Cripps and Mr. A. V. Alexander—to assist the Viceroy to obtain the widest measure of agreement as to the method of framing a Constitution, to set up a Constitution-making body and to create an Executive Council, having the support of the main Indian parties. After joint and individual discussions with Congress and League, which produced no agreement, the mission made its own proposals in May. These suggested that a Constituent Assembly for the 'Union of India' should be elected by the Provincial Assemblies, voting separately by religious communities, in the proportion of one representative for each million of the population. The Union should have authority in foreign affairs, defence and communications only. After a preliminary session of the Constituent Assembly, the provincial delegates were to meet in Sections A (Madras, Bombay, United Provinces, Bihar, Orissa, Central Provinces), B (Punjab, North West Frontier Province and Sind) and C (Bengal and Assam). The last two sections would have Muslim majorities. The sections were to determine whether the provinces concerned would take any provincial subjects in common as a Group. The Constitutions both of the Indian Union and of the Groups were to allow any province 'to call for a reconsideration of the terms of the Constitution' after ten years.

An interim government, representing the major parties, would be formed by the Viceroy to carry on the administration meanwhile. The paramountcy of His Majesty's Government over the states would lapse when the Indian Union came into being, and it would be for each state to negotiate its own future relationship with the Union.

On 6th June 1946 the Muslim League, satisfied that Muslim interests would be safeguarded by the grouping proposals, accepted the plan and agreed to join the Interim Government 'in the hope that it would ultimately result in the establishment of complete Pakistan'; and after obtaining an assurance from the

The Birth of Pakistan

Viceroy that 'we shall go ahead with the plan, so far as circumstances permit, if either party accepts'.[1] On 26th June the Congress accepted the Constitution-making part of the plan but refused to join the Interim Government. The Cabinet Mission then adjourned further discussions of the Interim Government until the elections for the Constituent Assembly had taken place; meanwhile the Viceroy formed a 'Caretaker Government' of civil servants.

The League regarded this as a direct breach of the promise given by the Viceroy that the plan would be proceeded with if either party accepted. It accused the Viceroy also of having promised the League that the Interim Government would consist of five Congress, five Muslim League and two other members, but of subsequently modifying this proposal to six Congress, five League, and three others. It strongly challenged Congress's good faith in accepting the long-term proposals, citing the statement of Pandit Nehru, the Congress President, on 10th July that 'The big probability is that there will be no grouping'.[2] The League now withdrew its acceptance of the proposals, called on all Muslims to renounce their titles, and decided on a campaign of 'Direct Action' to 'achieve Pakistan ... and to get rid of the present slavery under the British and contemplated future of Centre Hindu domination'.

Congress thereupon withdrew its objection to entering the Interim Government, and on 24th August the Viceroy's Council was re-formed, with its entire membership nominated by Congress, and with Pandit Nehru as its Vice-President. Thus the League's Direct Action campaign coincided with the formation of a predominantly Hindu central government. The result was unprecedented communal rioting. In Calcutta four thousand were killed, in Bihar five thousand, and in East Bengal there were fifty thousand homeless refugees.[3] In these circumstances

[1] Viceroy's letter to Mr. Jinnah, 4th June 1946, reproduced in Bannerjee, *Making of the Indian Constitution*, vol. i (Documents).
[2] Statement at Press Conference in Bombay. Text in Bannerjee, *Making of the Indian Constitution*, vol. i (Documents), p. 241.
[3] Statistics given by Sir Stafford Cripps in the House of Commons, 12th December 1946.

The Birth of Pakistan

Muslim interests could only suffer by their lack of representation at the Centre, and in October five League nominees, led by Liaquat Ali and including one Scheduled Caste Hindu, entered the Interim Government. The League, however, though its representatives were elected to the Constituent Assembly, refused to enter it. Meanwhile the Constituent Assembly showed no signs of dividing into the proposed Groups but proceeded to draft a Constitution.

It was admitted both by Congress and the British Government that such a Constitution could not be imposed on the unwilling Muslim-majority provinces. On 20th February 1947 Mr. Attlee, the British Prime Minister, made an important declaration. His Majesty's Government would grant full self-government to British India by June 1948 at latest, 'whether as a whole to some form of central government for British India or in some areas to the existing provincial governments, or in such other way as may seem most reasonable and in the best interests of the Indian people'. Lord Mountbatten would replace Lord Wavell as Viceroy in this final phase.

Mountbatten found a desperate situation: a central cabinet so divided as to be almost impotent; in the Punjab a Unionist government tottering under the attack of the Muslim League; in the North West Frontier a Muslim League civil disobedience campaign; and all over the country fierce communal clashes, whilst private armies formed for the final struggle for power. The civil services were bitterly divided by communalism and headed by dispirited Englishmen, anxious to retire. The British troops were already being repatriated, and the morale of the Indian Army was uncertain.

Mountbatten's solution, which he persuaded the British Government to adopt, was as decisive and drastic as might be expected from so distinguished a naval commander. On 3rd June the British Government accepted the principle of the Partition of India and undertook to hand over to the successor governments on 15th August full Dominion status, with the implicit right to secede from the Commonwealth. In the Punjab and Bengal the representatives of the Muslim and non-Muslim majority districts in the Provincial Assemblies were to vote separately on whether they wished to join the Indian Union or to form part of an autonomous 'Pakistan' constituent assembly. The Sind Legislative Assembly was to vote as a whole on the issue. The North West Frontier Province and Sylhet (the Muslim southern area of Assam) were to decide their future by referenda based on adult male suffrage; Baluchistan through a joint meeting of its representative institutions.

Both Congress and League accepted the plan. The result was as generally expected. The North West Frontier Province, Sind, Sylhet and Baluchistan voted for Pakistan. The western districts of the Punjab voted for Pakistan, the eastern districts for India. Similarly, in Bengal the eastern districts voted for Pakistan, and the western districts for India. Boundary commissions, each consisting of two non-Muslim and two Muslim representatives, with a British Chairman, Sir Cyril Radcliffe, were set up to define the exact boundaries of the new provinces of West and East Punjab and of West and East Bengal. In the meantime the Muslim-majority districts were regarded as part of Pakistan and the non-Muslim districts as part of India. In early July the Indian Independence Act passed through the British Parliament. The Dominions of India and Pakistan were created as from 15th August, and the whole authority in British India was transferred to their Constituent Assemblies. British paramountcy over the Indian states was terminated, and they were left free to make their own future arrangements with the new Dominion governments. On the recommendation of the Muslim League, Jinnah was appointed by the King as the first Governor General of the Dominion of Pakistan. On the recommendation of the Congress, Lord Mountbatten, the retiring Viceroy, was appointed first Governor General of the Dominion of India.

The Constituent Assembly of Pakistan met in its provisional capital of Karachi on 11th August. Jinnah was formally inaugurated as Governor General on the 15th. It was appropriate that his Prime Minister should be Liaquat Ali Khan who had served as Secretary of the Muslim League through the long years of Jinnah's presidency, and whom Jinnah had called his 'right hand' throughout the struggle for Pakistan.

The actions and motives of each of the three principal parties in these final negotiations—the Congress, the League and the British Government—will not be fully understood until the documents and memoirs of the period are published. The Congress, in retrospect, seems almost consciously to have thrown away the last chance of a United India. In June 1946 the League had agreed to come into a Constituent Assembly of the Union of India which should have its powers limited to foreign affairs, defence and communications; and immediately to enter an Interim Government in which Congress and League should have equal representation. Congress, while also agreeing to enter the Constituent Assembly, stood out of the Interim Government for the sake of an extra seat in it. The gap between Congress and League was then very narrow. Nehru made it unbridgeable by explaining to the Press that the Indian central government would control foreign trade, have powers of taxation and 'overall power to intervene in grave crisis, breakdown of the administration or economic breakdown or famine. The scope of the Centre, even though limited, inevitably grows because it cannot exist otherwise'.[1]

Congress at this time was irritated at the League's intransigence. Perhaps it still felt, as so many of its members privately stated, that Pakistan was a bluff which even the League leaders did not really believe practicable. Perhaps Nehru's statement was due to the conviction that a weak Centre would mean chaos, famine and Balkanization for the whole of India, and that even partition would be preferable to this. But to flaunt the threat of a strong federal government, with the inherent right to expand its functions, could hardly fail to drive the League out of the Constituent Assembly. For twenty years Muslim leaders, not only inside but outside the League, had made it clear that they could

---

[1] Statement at Press Conference in Bombay, 10th July 1946. Text in Bannerjee, *Making of the Indian Constitution*, vol. i, p. 241.

only accept a federal government whose powers were strictly limited, and in which the residuary powers would lie with its autonomous provinces.

The League has been criticized by some of its members for accepting in the Partition what Jinnah himself had previously referred to as a 'mutilated, moth-eaten and truncated Pakistan', without the industrial area of West Bengal, the river head waters of the East Punjab and the unexploited wealth of the Assam Valley. It is difficult to see how it could have made any other decision. The League's claim for the whole of Sind, the North West Frontier Province, Baluchistan, Punjab, Bengal and Assam would have created a professedly Muslim state, in which 48 per cent of the population of Eastern Pakistan and 38 per cent of the population of Western Pakistan would have been non-Muslims. As the Cabinet Mission stated: 'Every argument that can be used in favour of Pakistan can equally, in our view, be used in favour of the exclusion of the non-Muslim areas from Pakistan.'[1] Certainly the League was in no position to dispute this exclusion when the Congress made it the price of the Partition of India. League leaders were indeed distressed at having to leave forty million Muslims as a permanent minority in the Indian Dominion. But they believed that the existence of a similar non-Muslim minority in Pakistan would lead to mutual conventions of fair treatment.

The wisdom of the British Government's part in these final hectic negotiations is likely to be disputed for many years to come. The voluntary relinquishment of power over so vast a territory will surely be admired. The manner of leaving, however, may seem less praiseworthy. Most Pakistanis and many former British officers and civil servants regard the decision to advance the date of the transfer of power from June 1948 to August 1947 as a disastrous error of judgment. In two and a half months a new federal government had to be set up in Karachi, and the Services and assets of the Indian Government and of three

---

[1] Statement of 16th May 1946. Text in Bannerjee, *Making of the Indian Constitution*, vol. i, p. 140.

provincial governments divided. The Muslim League implored the Viceroy not to put forward the date, but the plan proceeded. On 15th August authority was handed over to provincial governments whose boundaries had not been defined, half of whose police and administrative services were in process of transfer, and which in the East Punjab had not even a temporary capital. In Bengal major disturbances were almost miraculously avoided by the joint efforts of Gandhi and of H. S. Suhrawardy, the retiring Premier. In the Punjab there was murder, abduction and arson in every district, which the authorities were totally incapable of checking. At the lowest estimate half a million people perished and twelve millions became homeless. And even after the wounds of the Punjab were checked by the complete evacuation of the surviving minorities, there remained the princely states, left in a vacuum by the sudden withdrawal of British paramountcy, to cause not only political but military conflict between the new Dominions.

The decision of the date of leaving was very difficult. There was strong pressure on the Viceroy and British Government from those who maintained that the existing administration could not survive until June 1948. Documents yet unpublished may suggest that postponement of the transfer of power would have led to disasters even worse than those which occurred. But in the meantime it is difficult to accept the view, which appears widely held in England, that the transfer of power was 'a political masterstroke . . . carried through without a major hitch'.[1] Such a picture does not seem convincing to the Punjabis, one of whom, a magistrate grown old in the British service, said to the writer, during the slaughter of the autumn of 1947: 'The British are a just people. They have left India in exactly the same state of chaos as they found it.'

[1] Professor C. H. Philips, *India*, pp. 149–50.

Part II
THE CREATION OF A STATE

NOTE

The study of Pakistan which is made in Part II covers the first two years of its independent existence, from August 1947 to August 1949.

CHAPTER VI

The Problems of Partition

The Division of India's Assets and Services—The Punjab
Disaster and the Refugees—The Accession of the States

When the Muslim League accepted the British Government's proposals of 3rd June 1947, and when the votes of the acceding provinces brought a Pakistan Constituent Assembly into being, the provisional Cabinet which was formed faced two obvious immediate problems. Firstly, Pakistan had to come to an agreement with the new Indian Privisional Government on the division of the assets and services of undivided India, and must set up a new Dominion administration to which they should be transferred. Secondly, the future of the Indian princely states must be decided, and the accession to Pakistan must, if possible, be obtained of those whose inclusion was imperative to her economy and security. But at the moment of her birth, Pakistan had to face a third, unexpected problem: the appalling communal disorders in the Punjab, which caused an influx of more than six million refugees.

To divide the personnel, assets, and liabilities of the Indian Empire in the seventy-two days which remained before the transfer of power, a Partition Council was set up in June 1947, consisting of two representatives each of India and of Pakistan and presided over by the Viceroy. The Council was assisted by ten Expert Committees, consisting equally of representatives of India and Pakistan, whose recommendations were submitted to the Council through a Steering Committee of senior civil servants.

One of the first tasks of the Council was to divide up the civil and defence services. Muslims in India and non-Muslims in Pakistan were given the right to opt for either Dominion: non-Muslims in India and Muslims in Pakistan had not the right to go to the other Dominion, except in the partitioned provinces of Bengal, the Punjab and Assam. The magnitude of the problem of partitioning the Indian Civil Service, railways, posts and telegraphs, customs, and other central services may be illustrated from one of them, the railways. Out of 925,000 railway employees, 73,000 had to be transferred from Pakistan to India and 83,500 from India to Pakistan, and this at a time when the efficient functioning of communications was one of the most vital factors in the success of the whole machinery of Partition.

The Expert Committees made proposals for the division of the assets and liabilities of every department of the Government of India. Typewriters, refrigerators, motor cars, office furniture, had to be itemized, valued and divided. In principle, Pakistan received $17\frac{1}{2}$ per cent of the joint assets. When an item could not be divided, she received a cash credit. Thus whilst India retained most of the unique institutions, museums, laboratories and research stations, Pakistan received financial compensation and the right to use them for a further five years.[1]

The financial arrangements caused some difficulty. Pakistan acquired $17\frac{1}{2}$ per cent of the uncovered debt and a similar proportion of the sterling balances in the United Kingdom. The division of cash balances was disputed and was ultimately settled by the intervention of Mr. Gandhi, who persuaded the Indian Government to hand over to Pakistan $17\frac{1}{2}$ per cent of them. A common currency and coinage was maintained until the Pakistan Reserve Bank was created in 1948.

There was disagreement on customs, excise and revenue duties. India's principle was that after Partition each Dominion

[1] Owing to the deterioration of inter-Dominion relations, Pakistan has been able to make little use of these institutions.

should keep what it collected. This was to the disadvantage of Pakistan, much of whose excisable goods such as sugar, matches and tobacco, came from India. She retaliated by placing an export duty on jute.

The division of the defence services and of war material formed a special problem. The immediate disentanglement before 15th August of Muslims and non-Muslims from every unit was impossible. Moreover, this would have seriously disorganized the Punjab Boundary Force which had been created to maintain order in that province at the time of Partition. A Joint Defence Council was therefore set up, with Lord Mountbatten as neutral Chairman and with a British Supreme Commander as its executive agent, to partition and transfer the defence forces and material by 1st April 1948. This was the least successful part of the machinery of Partition. By far the greater portion of the military stores was in India, as were all the arsenals. As inter-Dominion relations rapidly deteriorated during the Punjab massacres and the Kashmir fighting, India became very reluctant to send weapons and ammunition to Pakistan which, she apprehended, might be used against her. The British Supreme Commander's headquarters was closed on 1st December 1947 before any appreciable quantity of the material had been transferred.

Pakistan had chosen as its provisional capital Karachi, the principal city of Sind and chief seaport of the area which now comprised Western Pakistan. Accommodation was arranged for the more important ministries in the Sind Secretariat, and in tents and barracks. Subordinate offices were set up in Lahore, and Army General Headquarters at Rawalpindi. From Delhi alone twenty-five thousand government employees and their families, with sixty thousand tons of personal baggage, had to be moved to Karachi. The special train service which was started for them had to be suspended owing to derailment, looting and murder of passengers on their way through the Punjab. Indian commercial planes were next chartered, but were soon requisitioned by the Government of India for the transport of its own employees and refugees from Pakistan. British airlines provided forty planes which moved seven thousand Pakistani government servants. When conditions seemed safer rail transfer was restarted with armed escorts, but even then three trains were attacked and many passengers lost their lives.

The partition of the services, assets and liabilities of the divided provinces was effected through joint councils similar to that at the Centre. In the Punjab, the main difficulties were in the East, which had to set up a new administration and find a new capital. In Bengal, although West Bengal retained the provincial secretariat at Calcutta, East Bengal and that part of Assam which came to Pakistan were able to make use of the skeleton headquarters of Dacca, which had been a provincial capital forty years earlier. An Arbitral Tribunal had been created, under the presidency of a former British Chief Justice of India, to settle disputes arising from the Partition. It was not called upon to make any awards between India and Pakistan, but certain disputes between the divided provinces were referred to it. The Expert Committees consisted mostly of men who had worked together in the same Services for many years, and who were capable both of compromise and quick decision. The failures of the Partition machinery in the defence and financial arrangements were not inherent, but were caused by political events which were not foreseen when it was created.

The improvisation by Pakistan in seventy-two days of a federal government in a new capital, in spite of interrupted communications, was an excellent achievement. What was even more remarkable was the success of that government in withstanding the shock of the Punjab catastrophe.

In order to understand the disaster of the autumn of 1947 in the Punjab it is necessary to recollect the history of the province, and in particular that of the Sikhs. The Sikhs were originally disciples of Guru Nanak, a fifteenth-century mystic who endeavoured to reconcile the teachings of Hinduism and Islam. Persecuted by the later Moguls, partly for their allegiance to an unsuccessful claimant to the empire, they became a military community with certain distinctive outward characteristics, such as long hair and the obligation to carry a knife or sword. In a triangular struggle with invading Afghans and the declining Mogul power they established themselves at the end of the eighteenth century under Ranjit Singh as rulers of the greater part of the Punjab. The Sikhs were defeated and the Punjab annexed by the East India Company in 1849, but they retained their pride as its last independent rulers and kept up their martial traditions in the Indian Army. They numbered in 1947 less than four millions out of the province's population of twenty-eight millions, and were fairly evenly distributed between the eastern and western districts. With long memories of warfare against the Muslims, they were bitterly opposed to the movement for Pakistan, which would place their richest lands under a Muslim government and would lessen their influence by dispersing them between two Dominions.

In March 1947 the Punjab Unionist Ministry of Khizr Hayat Khan, a coalition based on the support of most of the Hindus and Sikhs and a few Muslims in the Provincial Assembly, resigned in face of the vigorous agitation of the Muslim League. The Governor, Sir Evan Jenkins, took charge of the administration. There followed fierce clashes between the Sikhs, who demonstrated shouting 'Death to Pakistan', and the Muslim Leaguers, who were determined to gain control of the Government. These led to bloody communal riots in which, particularly in the Rawalpindi Division, the Sikhs and Hindus suffered much more severely than the Muslims.

With the announcement in June that the Punjab would be partitioned, it seems from the speeches of their leaders, such as Master Tara Singh, that the Sikhs prepared their revenge. Those living in the rich canal colonies of the West Punjab were to march out to the Indian border, causing destruction and dislocation on their way. Those in the East Punjab were to slaughter and expel their Muslim neighbours, in alliance with the militant Hindu organization, the Rashtriya Swayam Sevak Sangha.

The Punjab Government, which remained under Governor's

F

81

rule until the Partition, discovered at least part of this plan, as well as a plot to assassinate Jinnah, and reported it to the Viceroy. The latter was strongly urged by the Muslim members of his Executive Council to arrest the Sikh leaders, but after consultation with the Governor, did not do so.

At the beginning of August widespread disorders broke out all over the Punjab which intensified as the date of Partition drew near. The Pakistanis produce considerable evidence to show that these were started by the Sikhs and the Rashtriya Swayam Sevak Sangha. They do not deny, however, that there was immediate retaliation by the Muslims.[1] Whole sections of Lahore, Amritsar, Sheikhupara, and indeed of most of the principal cities of the Punjab were in flames. In the villages armed bands plundered, burned, massacred and raped. Thousands of women, Muslim, Hindu and Sikh, were abducted, never to be seen again by their relatives. The Punjab Boundary Force, containing both Muslim and non-Muslim troops and commanded by British senior officers, was utterly incapable of maintaining the peace. Its troops refused to fire on members of their own communities, and it was disbanded, leaving the armies of Pakistan and India each responsible for its own area. The governments of both West and East Punjab were thoroughly disorganized by the transfer of civil officers and police which was still in process. East Punjab had no capital, and its principal departments were quartered in four different cities.

Spontaneously on both sides of the border, the minorities collected together in improvised camps or, placing their favourite belongings in bullock carts, marched towards the frontier. All

---

[1] Documents published by the West Punjab Government as appendices to *The Sikh Plan* and *The Sikhs in Action* (Lahore, 1948) seem strong evidence that the disturbances of August 1947 (but not those of March 1947) were started by the Sikhs. Accounts published in India give a quite different picture (e.g. K. L. Gauba, *Inside Pakistan*, Delhi, 1948). Also, evidence given at the Mamdot Enquiry in Lahore in 1949, as reported by *Dawn* of 22nd October, indicated that Muslim League leaders had purchased hand grenades, jeeps and other war material in 1946. Until the official papers and memoirs of the period are published nothing conclusive can be written on these events.

along the roads they were ambushed and butchered. Those who travelled by rail fared little better, for the trains were derailed and their occupants cut to pieces.

The Governments of India and Pakistan, despairing of stopping the slaughter, decided at the end of August to assist the complete evacuation of Muslims from East Punjab and of non-Muslims from West Punjab. A Joint Military Evacuation Organization was set up at Lahore. Mixed guards were provided for the refugee camps and armed escorts for foot, railway and motor convoys. But the trouble could not be confined to the Punjab. There was a savage outbreak of murder and looting in Delhi itself, and one hundred thousand Muslims, civil servants, professors, coolies and camelmen together, took shelter in the Purana Qila, an ancient Pathan fort, and demanded to be evacuated to Pakistan. The worst fate of all was reserved for the Muslims in the Sikh states of East Punjab. Here they had no hope of the protection of officers of the Indian Army and of the Indian Civil Service who in the Punjab were trying, however ineffectively, to curb the communal passions. Kapurthala State had a majority of Muslim inhabitants. All were killed or driven out. Those who survived, harassed by guerrilla groups, without food and sleep, encountered unprecedented floods along the road. More even were drowned than slaughtered, and very few reached Pakistan.

The Pakistan Government estimate that in the exchange of populations, excluding those from Kashmir, approximately 6,500,000 refugees came into Pakistan. Of these 5,200,000 came from the East Punjab and the East Punjab states, 360,000 from Delhi Province and the remainder from other parts of Northern India. They believe that about 500,000 Muslims lost their lives or were abducted. On the other side of the balance sheet, it is estimated that about 5,500,000 Hindus and Sikhs (including those who were killed) left Western Pakistan. The total increase in Pakistan's population was therefore about 1,000,000.[1]

[1] A Government of India census at the end of 1948 enumerated 4,400,000 refugees from Western Pakistan in India. In addition, in June 1949, the

The Problems of Partition

The economic dislocation caused was great. The West Punjab obtained a considerable surplus of agriculturalists, weavers, potters, shoemakers and other artisans. It lost, on the other hand, probably 80 per cent of its traders and 90 per cent of the sweepers, who were responsible for sanitation. In the villages the agricultural credit system disappeared with the Hindu moneylender. In the market towns it was impossible for the peasant to sell his crop because the Hindu wholesaler had left. In the cities the banks were closed because accountants and clerks had almost all been Hindus.

Jinnah and Liaquat Ali moved to Lahore, the capital of the West Punjab, and a Pakistan Ministry of Refugees was created to assist and supervise the work of the Provincial Government. The refugees on arrival were fed and clothed as far as resources would allow. Middle-class women came out of purdah to nurse the sick and wounded. A branch of the Red Cross was organized, and British and American relief agencies sent personnel and supplies. After feeding the refugees, the most urgent task was to put the cultivators on the farm land vacated by the Hindus and Sikhs, lest the country's richest source of food should be imperilled. Agricultural land was rapidly allotted and loans advanced until the first harvest came in. There was not room for all in the Punjab, and several hundred thousand refugees were sent to Sind where there was more opportunity to bring new land under cultivation.

In industry and commerce, resettlement and reorganization were more intricate. The urban property of Hindus and Sikhs who had left was allotted to refugees temporarily, and the rents held for the absentee owners by a High Court judge who was appointed as Custodian of Refugee Property. Bank clerks and accountants were hurriedly trained in night classes. Untrained auxiliary nurses were enrolled to maintain the hospitals. The Co-

---

Government of India estimated that 1,600,000 refugees from Eastern Pakistan were in India. The number of Muslims who had migrated from India to Pakistan at that time was given as 5,800,000. No Indian estimate has been given of the number of non-Muslims killed in 1947.

84

The Problems of Partition

operatives played an enterprising and patriotic part in purchasing the rice and wheat crops and in starting general retail stores in the district towns.

There was inevitable corruption and unfairness; for small officials had great responsibility in the allotment of valuable lands and property. There was squabbling between provinces, each fearful of being submerged by the flood of refugees. But by the end of 1948 the refugee camps were empty. Somehow six and a half million refugees had been absorbed in the economy of Western Pakistan. Many might still be unemployed or partly employed, living on charity. Industry had not recovered its efficiency. On all sides there was the grumbling and dissatisfaction invariably found among émigrés. But Pakistan had survived: had indeed gained in strength. For if at the time of Partition there had been any doubt in Pakistani minds, any wish for ultimate reunion with India, it was buried for ever now with the Punjab dead.

At the transfer of power, all the Muslim majority districts of the divided provinces of the Punjab and Bengal had been regarded as temporarily part of Pakistan, and the non-Muslim majority districts as temporarily part of India, pending the decision of Boundary Commissions which had been set up with instructions 'to demarcate the boundaries of the two parts of Bengal (Punjab) on the basis of ascertaining the contiguous areas of Muslims and non-Muslims. In doing so, it will also take into account other factors'. In both the Bengal and Punjab Commissions there was disagreement between Muslim and non-Muslim representatives, and in each the decision was given by the Chairman, Sir Cyril Radcliffe, in Awards published on 18th August. The Punjab Award caused much indignation in Pakistan, for it gave the greater part of the Muslim majority district of Gurdaspur to the East Punjab, thus allowing India access to Kashmir, which had not yet decided whether to accede to India or Pakistan. The Awards were, however, accepted.

The boundaries of that part of Pakistan which had been created out of British India were now settled. But there remained

85

to be decided the future of the Indian states. The Indian Empire had included at the time of Partition not only the provinces of British India, with a population of 294,000,000 but in addition over 500 states, varying in size from a few thousand to several million inhabitants, and with a total population of 89,000,000. The rulers of the states, the Nizam, the Maharajahs and Nawabs, were mostly hereditary autocrats, administering their own laws, imposing and collecting taxes, and in several states maintaining armies. Each prince, however, acknowledged the paramountcy of the British Crown, which was alone responsible for the foreign relations of the states, and which had the right to intervene in a state in case of serious misgovernment. British relations with the states were maintained through the Viceroy in his capacity as Crown Representative. Under the terms of the Indian Independence Act, British paramountcy lapsed on 15th August. The states were therefore in theory free to accede either to India or to Pakistan or to remain independent. Mountbatten, however, while still Viceroy, urged the princes very strongly to join either India or Pakistan, whichever might be contiguous to their territories and desired by their subjects, and to sign a standard form of accession, placing responsibility for defence, foreign relations and communications under one of the Dominion Governments.[1]

Few of the states saw any hope of independent survival. The great majority, having Hindu rulers and Hindu subjects and being surrounded by Indian territory, acceded to India. Others, predominantly Muslim and adjacent to Pakistan, acceded to that Dominion. Of these Bahawalpur, with a population of 1,340,000, Khairpur (300,000) and Kalat (250,000) were the most important. In all, excluding the disputed accessions, six states acceded to Pakistan with a total population of about 2,000,000. The tribal areas of the North West Frontier, controlled through political agents, all signified through their various councils or

---

[1] Mountbatten's address to Conference of Princes and Ministers, 25th July 1947. Text in Bannerjee, *Making of the Indian Constitution*, vol. i, p. 540.

The Problems of Partition

chiefs their desire to join Pakistan and brought a further 2,380,000 inhabitants into the Dominion. But the future of three states caused bitter controversy between India and Pakistan.

Junagadh was a state on the coast of Kathiawar, the majority of whose 800,000 inhabitants were Hindu, but whose ruler was a Muslim. In September 1947 he acceded to Pakistan, although his territory was nowhere contiguous to that Dominion. A party of his subjects rebelled against him and invited the Indian Army into the state. India held a plebiscite whose results were over 90 per cent in favour of accession to India, and annexed Junagadh. Pakistan's protest to the Security Council has still to be considered by the United Nations Commission for India and Pakistan.

The Junagadh incident aroused strong feeling in Pakistan. Yet, although the insult was resented, many Pakistanis admitted that the majority of the state's population, being Hindus, probably wished for accession to India. In the state of Jammu and Kashmir the position was almost exactly opposite. Of a population of 4,000,000, over 3,000,000 were Muslims but the ruler was a Hindu. Faced by a successful rebellion among his subjects and an invasion by Muslim tribesmen, he acceded to India in October 1947 despite a Standstill Agreement with Pakistan. Neither Pakistan nor a considerable part of his subjects acknowledged the accession, and, as we shall see in a subsequent chapter, the result was an undeclared localized war in Kashmir between armies of India and Pakistan. Kashmir was symbolized by the 'K' in Pakistan. Three of the great rivers of the Punjab had their origins in the state. Its borders marched with China and Tibet, and were only separated by a few miles from Russia. So vital seems its possession for economic and political security to Pakistan that her whole foreign and defence policy has largely revolved round the Kashmir dispute.

After Kashmir came the Hyderabad affair. Hyderabad was by far the largest state in India. Of a population of 16,000,000, only 2,000,000 were Muslims, and the territory was entirely surrounded by the Indian provinces of Bombay, Madras and the

87

The Problems of Partition

Central Provinces. The Nizam made every effort to preserve his independence, flying in foreign armaments through Karachi. He concluded a Standstill Agreement for one year with India. But before it expired, in August 1948, India, after complaining that her border villages were being plundered by armed Muslim bands, sent her troops into the state, defeated the Hyderabad State forces and eventually obtained the Nizam's accession.[1] Pakistan could hardly hope that Hyderabad would accede to her, for there was no communication by sea or land; but Muslims had a sentimental and cultural interest in the state. The Nizam's rule was a relic and symbol of the Mogul Empire, and his court and university were a centre of Urdu learning. As rumours of a massacre of Muslims reached Karachi after the Indian victory, crowds clamoured around the Prime Minister's house demanding action. Pakistan could only officially pursue the matter at Lake Success; but the incident added to her bitterness against India, whom she accused of hypocritically taking a legalistic stand over Kashmir before the Security Council, while using quite contrary arguments over Junagadh and Hyderabad.

[1] The Nizam in a broadcast on 23rd September 1948, after the Indian occupation of Hyderabad, stated that he had wished to come to a friendly settlement with India, but had been prevented by his ministers.

CHAPTER VII

The Political and Constitutional Framework

Under Section 8 of the Indian Independence Act, the Government of India Act of 1935 became, with certain adaptations, the working Constitution of Pakistan. At the Centre, the Constituent Assembly was given two separate functions, firstly to prepare a Constitution, and secondly to act as a Federal Legislative Assembly or Parliament until that Constitution came into effect. The Constituent Assembly can amend the Indian Independence Act or the Government of India Act, and no act of the British Parliament can be extended to Pakistan without legislation by it. Pakistan remains a Dominion of the British Commonwealth, but has the right to secede from it. Although her Governor General is formally appointed by the King, he is nominated by the Pakistan Cabinet. Pakistan may therefore be described as a sovereign independent state.

The government of Pakistan is carried on by a Cabinet which is collectively responsible to the Constituent Assembly. The Governor General has no individual discretion, and is always

The Political and Constitutional Framework

presumed to act on the advice of his ministers. He may promulgate ordinances, but these are subject to repeal by the Constituent Assembly. The Dominion is a federation, and the Government of India Act defines those subjects which are the responsibility of the Central Government and those which are the responsibility of the provinces. The central judiciary consists of a Federal Court of Pakistan with original, appellate and advisory functions. Its judges are appointed by the Governor General.

The Dominion consists of:

(i) The Governor's provinces of West Punjab, Sind, North West Frontier Province and East Bengal. Each has an elected Legislative Assembly,[1] and is normally governed by a cabinet of ministers responsible to that Assembly. In exceptional circumstances, however, the Governor of the province, who is appointed by the Governor General of Pakistan, may be directed by the latter to take over the administration. The provinces are represented in the Pakistan Constituent Assembly by delegates from their own Legislative Assemblies, elected in the proportion of one for each million inhabitants of the province.

(ii) The states which have acceded to Pakistan, namely, Bahawalpur, Khairpur, Kalat, Makran, Kharan and Las Bela. These are autonomous, with the exception of defence, foreign relations and communications, which have been delegated to the Centre. The rulers of the states maintain relations with Pakistan through the Ministry of States and Frontier Regions. In the two largest of them, Pakistan officers have been lent to serve as Prime Ministers.

(iii) Baluchistan. Baluchistan is governed by an Agent of the Governor General, with the aid of local nominated advisers. Representative institutions are at present being planned.

(iv) Tribal territories. Relations with the tribal chiefs and councils of the North West Frontier are maintained through the Governor of the North West Frontier Province as the Agent of

[1] East Bengal has a Legislative Council also, an Upper House elected on a much more restricted franchise than the Legislative Assembly.

The Political and Constitutional Framework

the Governor General. The primitive peoples of the Chittagong Hill Tracts are similarly the responsibility of the Governor General through the agency of the Governor of East Bengal.

(v) Karachi, chosen by the Constituent Assembly as the federal capital, is governed by an administrator, responsible to the Minister of the Interior of the Pakistan Government.

In the provinces the administrative machinery remains identical to that of British India. Each province consists of divisions, further divided into districts, in which the Divisional Commissioner and District Magistrate (also known as Deputy Commissioner or Collector) have both revenue and magisterial functions. Local self-government continues under district boards and municipalities. The government of the states remains generally autocratic.

In the senior ranks of the Indian Services at the time of Partition Muslims were considerably outnumbered by non-Muslims. Yet the Pakistan Government had not only to continue to man the provincial administrations but to create an entire new central government. To meet the emergency, British officers of the Indian Services were encouraged to continue with Pakistan. Former British officers of the Indian Civil Service were appointed as Governors of three out of the four provinces, as Permanent Secretaries of four of the federal ministries, and in many other senior positions. British officers were also retained as heads of the Army, Navy and Air Force. Nationalization has, however, been taking place. The British Governors of the West Punjab and of the North West Frontier Province resigned in 1949 and were replaced by Pakistanis, and it is hoped to dispense with British officers in the army by the end of 1950, except as technical advisers.

The present population of Pakistan can only be estimated. Since the last census of 1941, allowance must be made both for refugee movements and for the increase of $1\frac{1}{2}$ per cent per annum which was normal in British India. The Government of Pakistan estimated the population in 1948 as:

East Bengal	46,720,000
Baluchistan (districts)	560,000
N.W.F.P. (districts)	3,200,000
Sind (including Karachi)	5,180,000
West Punjab	19,740,000
Bahawalpur State	1,480,000
Other States and Tribal Areas	3,380,000
Total population of Pakistan	80,260,000[1]

This population is exceeded only by that of four countries in the world—China, India, U.S.S.R. and U.S.A.

The Constituent Assembly is a body of only seventy members, many of whom are ministers or important leaders in the provinces. In the critical months immediately after Partition, therefore, while the new provincial governments were being set up, it was not possible for the Assembly to meet. The Cabinet and the Governor General had the heavy task of holding together and welding together very different elements, at a time of great strain, and with little opportunity to meet the elected representatives. East Bengal, which had an absolute majority of the Dominion's population, was separated from the capital by over a thousand miles of Indian territory. Its border with Burma and its rice economy linked it to South East Asia. Sind, on the other hand, had always stood a little apart from the Indian subcontinent and had close ties with the Arab countries of the Middle East. Now it was aggrieved by the loss of its capital to the Central Government, and apprehensive of the influx of Punjab refugees. The Pathans of the North West Frontier came from the same stock as the Afghans, and some of their leaders had urged them to form a separate 'Pathanistan'. The West Punjab was so preoccupied with its refugees as to be able to give little appreciation to the problems of Pakistan as a whole.

The heaviest part of the burden in the first year of Pakistan

[1] Table prepared for *Pakistan*, British Industries Fair Review, London, 1949.

The Political and Constitutional Framework

was carried by Jinnah himself. He was far more than Governor General. He was the Quaid-i-Azam, the 'Great Leader' who had brought the state into being, and as such could admonish and persuade the provinces as none of his ministers could do. After supervising the immediate refugee problems in Lahore, he toured the other provinces, speaking bluntly and soberly. The first duty of a government, he told the Constituent Assembly before its members dispersed to their provinces in August, was to maintain law and order; the second to root out corruption. The minorities must be treated with absolute fairness. 'You may belong to any religion or caste or creed; that has nothing to do with the business of the State.' Provincialism, he warned the Bengalis, was liable to be the biggest curse to Pakistan. 'As long as you do not throw off this poison in our body politic, you will never be able to weld yourself, mould yourself, galvanize yourself into a true nation.'

His influence was steadying in a time of fierce excitement. At the end of October he addressed a huge open-air meeting in Lahore which was clamouring for intervention in Kashmir. He deliberately refrained from mentioning Kashmir and instead advised his audience to concentrate their efforts on helping the refugees, to avoid retaliation, exercise restraint, and protect the minority communities. He urged the students to stick to their studies, and the Muslims who were still in India to give unflinching loyalty to their own government. And he repeatedly laid down the challenge: 'it is easier to go to jail or fight for freedom than to run a government'.[1]

Jinnah was over seventy and in poor health. In addition to being Governor General, he was President of the Constituent Assembly and the ultimate authority in the Muslim League. In the last instance all major decisions of the Government and the party came to him. He died of heart failure in September 1948. He had worked himself to death, but had contributed more than any other man to Pakistan's survival.

[1] Quotations from *Speeches by Quaid-i-Azam M. A. Jinnah as Governor-General*. Published by Pakistan Government, Karachi, 1948.

The Political and Constitutional Framework

The Cabinet chose as his successor Khwaja Nazimuddin, the Prime Minister of East Bengal. Nazimuddin had had long experience as a provincial minister under the constitutions of 1919 and 1935. He was an old Leaguer, religious, fair-minded and affable. It was a wise choice, not only for his evident qualities as a shrewd and popular constitutional Governor General, but as a sign that the needs of remote East Bengal would not be forgotten by the Central Government.

The death of Jinnah left a greater responsibility with the Cabinet. It fell most heavily perhaps on the Prime Minister, the Minister for Foreign Affairs and the Finance Minister.

The Prime Minister, Minister of Defence, and Minister for States and Frontier Regions, Liaquat Ali Khan, was born in the East Punjab in 1895, and educated at Aligarh and Oxford. Many years as a member of the Legislative Assemblies of the United Provinces and of undivided India have made him a capable parliamentarian, and his experience as Secretary of the Muslim League from 1936 to 1947 has given him a strong hold on the party. Both his vision and his executive ability were marked in the 'Poor Man's Budget' which he introduced in 1947 when Finance Member of the Viceroy's Council, and though himself the son of a Nawab, he proclaims 'Islamic Socialism' as the goal of Pakistan. His outstanding characteristic as Prime Minister has been the serenity with which he has confronted both political crises and mass demonstrations. A weaker or more emotional man might not have been able to avoid war with India.

Sir Mohammad Zafrullah Khan was a natural choice as Foreign Minister. Born in 1893, he qualified as a barrister of Lincoln's Inn in London, and afterwards served in the highest positions in the Government of India. He held in turn the Commerce, Law and Supplies portfolios in the Viceroy's Council, was a judge of the Federal Court from 1941 to 1947, and represented India in China and at several international conferences. As Foreign Minister of Pakistan, he has handled with dignity, ability and great eloquence his country's case in the Kashmir dispute. His effective championship before the United

The Political and Constitutional Framework

Nations of the Arabs in Palestine and North Africa has done much to strengthen Pakistan's links with the Middle East. Zafrullah has admirably presented to the outside world a Pakistan which, though young, has already consistent and serious principles of foreign policy.

Yet neither the confident leadership of Liaquat nor the capable foreign policy of Zafrullah would have been effective had they not been based on a stable internal economy. Balanced budgets, both in 1948 and 1949, were the contribution of the Finance Minister, Ghulam Muhammad. Ghulam Muhammad, in contrast to most other members of the Cabinet, was a civil servant who rose to high rank in the Government of India. A Punjabi, born of a poor family in 1895, he was educated at Aligarh and was one of the first Muslims to be taken into the Indian Audit Department. He eventually became Finance Minister of Hyderabad State, a knight and a director of Tatas, the great Indian iron and steel company. He has not only financial acumen but great powers of persuasion. He has probably been the most successful of the ministers in negotiations with India, where he retains many friends.

Bengal has three representatives in the Cabinet. Khwaja Shahabuddin, brother of the Governor General, holds the Interior, Information and Refugee portfolios. For several years Muslim League Chief Whip and a provincial minister in Bengal, he is the most important link between Eastern and Western Pakistan. Fazlur Rahman, Minister for Commerce and Education, is a lawyer who was also a minister in undivided Bengal. J. N. Mandal, Minister of Law and Labour, is the only non-Muslim in the Cabinet. He was the President in Bengal of Dr. Ambedkar's Scheduled Castes Federation and, with the approval of Ambedkar, joined the Pakistan Government when his leader became a minister in the Indian Government.

Sind is represented by Pirzada Abdus Sattar, Minister for Food, Agriculture and Health. The North West Frontier by Abdur Rab Nishtar, who was once a distinguished Congressman and is still a distinguished poet. In 1949 a Minister without

Portfolio was added to the Cabinet to co-ordinate Kashmir affairs. He is Mushtaq Ahmed Gurmani, a former Prime Minister of Bahawalpur State. Gurmani, born a Nawab, is a Punjabi who has many of Liaquat's characteristics of equability and common sense. The average age of the Cabinet is under fifty.[1]

In the Constituent Assembly, to which the Cabinet is responsible, all the Muslim seats except one are held by members of the Muslim League. The League is open to all Muslims, male or female, above the age of eighteen, on payment of two annas per annum. Each province sends delegates to the All Pakistan Muslim League Council, which annually elects a President. The latter appoints his own Working Committee. The All Pakistan League Council consists of about four hundred and fifty members and the Working Committee of about twenty-one members. A similar procedure is followed in provincial and district organizations. In elections, both to central and provincial assemblies, the League 'ticket' is issued to candidates chosen by sub-committees of the All Pakistan and Provincial Councils.

Until 1947 the League comprehended all Muslims who were in favour of Pakistan, and it had no very clear economic programme. Since the establishment of Pakistan, however, it has been preparing a programme of agrarian reforms. If, as is expected, the next elections are on the basis of adult suffrage, it is likely that the League platform will be definitely radical. The present President, Choudhury Khaliquzzaman, the former League leader in the United Provinces, is particularly interested in Pan-Islamic movements. Foreign policy may also, therefore, become a more important part of the League's programme.

The League's continued cohesion as the only important Muslim party has been largely due to the need for Muslim solidarity whilst Pakistan's economy was endangered by the influx of

---

[1] Abdur Rab Nishtar became Governor of the West Punjab in August 1949. He was replaced as Communications Minister by Sardar Bahadur Khan, who is also a Pathan. At the same time two other new ministers were appointed, Chaudhry Nazir Ahmed, a Punjabi, as Industries Minister, and Dr. Mallik of Bengal as Health Minister.

refugees and whilst her political existence was threatened by her conflict with India over Kashmir. Much of the energy and interest which might otherwise have been directed by political workers towards social and economic reforms have been spent in organizing home guards and relief for refugees both from the Punjab and Kashmir.

Yet, though there is no organized Muslim political opposition, there are critical groups within the League. On the left is Iftikharuddin, once a minister in the West Punjab, a former Congressman and by repute a former Communist. Iftikharuddin comes of a wealthy and politically prominent Punjab family and owns the *Pakistan Times*, which criticizes the Government for joining the Anglo-American bloc rather than coming to an understanding with Russia. He is young, Oxford-educated and a capable speaker. He may have a considerable following among the West Punjab refugees, for he resigned from the Provincial Government because, as he alleged, it would not sufficiently disturb vested interests in their favour. On the right are the religious critics, of whom the most influential and moderate is Maulana Shabbir Osmani. The Maulanas criticize the Government for not being sufficiently Islamic and urge the enforcement of the laws of the Shariat, as in the early days of Islam, which would prohibit the lending of money on interest and impose very severe penalties for social offences.

The only Muslim in the Constituent Assembly who is not a Leaguer is Abdul Ghaffar Khan, the leader of the Khudai Khidmatgars (Servants of God) of the Frontier, the party which, in alliance with the Congress, twice formed ministries in the North West Frontier Province. Abdul Ghaffar is at present in jail, under suspicion of plotting against Pakistan with the tribal leader, the Fakir of Ipi, and, as some Pakistanis say, with India. He has probably lost much of his influence since his opposition to the participation of the people of the Frontier in the Kashmir war, which was generally regarded by them as a crusade.

The most effective political critic of the Government is H. S. Suhrawardy, the last premier of undivided Bengal. Brilliant and imaginative, if somewhat mercurial, he fell out of favour with the League for proposing immediately before Partition that Bengal should remain united as a sovereign independent state. After Partition, he remained in India and, working with Gandhi, did much to protect the minorities. He has recently migrated to Pakistan, where his criticism of governmental 'inefficiency' and his capable legal defence of certain political *détenus* would probably make him the natural leader of the opposition if he could obtain a place in the Constituent Assembly.

The twelve million Hindus who are still in Pakistan, almost all in East Bengal, are represented in the Constituent Assembly by twelve members of the Congress Party and one representative of the Scheduled Castes Federation. The Congressmen have played their unhappy part with dignity, always affirming their loyalty to the State in making their complaints. For many years predominant in government services, in commerce and education in Bengal, and indeed having been one of the most powerful forces behind the Indian National Congress itself, they now find themselves excluded both from the Pakistan and East Bengal Governments. As long as the Pakistan and Indian armies remain resting uneasily on their arms in Kashmir, it is likely that Congressmen will be too suspect to be included either in the Pakistan or provincial cabinets. The best that can be said is that in East Bengal the Hindus, though they have lost influence, continue to maintain their shops and worship in their temples, seldom molested. The contrast is severe in the West Punjab, where no Sikh and only a few thousand Hindus remain.

The Scheduled Castes, low-caste Hindus who had been granted separate representation by the Constitution of 1935, have four representatives in the Constituent Assembly, three of whom are Congressmen and the fourth, the Minister J. N. Mandal, a member of the Scheduled Castes Federation. The Scheduled Castes have received special benefits from the Pakistan Government. Six per cent of the positions in the central services are reserved for them, and an annual allotment of five hundred thousand rupees is made for their education.

The Political and Constitutional Framework

The Christians at the time of Partition suffered considerable hardship in the West Punjab, where incoming Muslim refugees complained that Christians had looted them in the East Punjab. There are still four hundred thousand of them in the West Punjab, but skilful leadership by S. P. Singha, the former Speaker of the Punjab Assembly, has improved their position, and they are included in a special reservation of 5 per cent of the positions in the Services for the minorities in that province. They have no representation in the Constituent Assembly and they not unreasonably ask for separate electorates until 'the Muslim League as the national political body is substituted by one or more political organizations open to all communities'.[1]

The most tranquil minority are undoubtedly the Parsees, who neither in India nor Pakistan have ever claimed separate communal representation. Persian by origin, their religion in no way affects their politics, and in Karachi and Lahore, though few in number, they have usefully filled many gaps left in commerce and industry by the departing Hindus.

Although the Constituent Assembly has not yet prepared a draft Constitution, it passed in March 1949 a resolution on the 'Aims and Objects of the Constitution', which was described by the Prime Minister as 'the most important occasion in the life of this country, next in importance only to the achievement of independence'. Not only the resolution itself but the debate on it are of great interest as illustrating the political philosophy of the present Government of Pakistan and of its principal critics.

The text of the Resolution, which was moved by the Prime Minister, was:

'In the name of Allah, the Beneficent, the Merciful;

'WHEREAS sovereignty over the entire universe belongs to God Almighty alone and the authority which He has delegated to the

---

[1] *Safeguards for Minorities suggested by the All Pakistan Christian League*, Lahore, 1949.

State of Pakistan through its people for being exercised within the limit prescribed by Him is a sacred trust;

'This Constituent Assembly representing the people of Pakistan resolves to frame a constitution for the sovereign independent State of Pakistan;

'WHEREIN the State shall exercise its powers and authority through the chosen representatives of the people;

'WHEREIN the principles of democracy, freedom, equality, tolerance and social justice, as enunciated by Islam, shall be fully observed;

'WHEREIN the Muslims shall be enabled to order their lives in the individual and collective spheres in accord with the teachings and requirements of Islam as set out in the Holy Quran and the Sunna;[1]

'WHEREIN adequate provision shall be made for the minorities freely to profess and practise their religions and develop their cultures;

'WHEREBY the territories now included in or in accession with Pakistan and such other territories as may hereafter be included in or accede to Pakistan shall form a Federation wherein the units will be autonomous with such boundaries and limitations on their powers and authority as may be prescribed;

'WHEREIN shall be guaranteed fundamental rights including equality of status, of opportunity and before law, social, economic and political justice, and freedom of thought, expression, belief, faith, worship and association, subject to law and public morality.

'WHEREIN adequate provision shall be made to safeguard the legitimate interests of minorities and backward and depressed classes;

'WHEREIN the independence of the judiciary shall be fully secured;

'WHEREIN the integrity of the territories of the Federation, its independence and all its rights including its sovereign rights on land, sea and air shall be safeguarded;

[1] Traditions of the Holy Prophet.

The Political and Constitutional Framework

'So that the people of Pakistan may prosper and attain their rightful and honoured place amongst the nations of the World and make their full contribution towards international peace and the progress and happiness of humanity.'[1]

The resolution was adopted without a division after an amendment by the Congress to delete the preamble had been defeated by twenty-one votes to ten.

The Congress objections to the resolution were stated by Mr. B. K. Dutta. 'Politics and religion belong to two different regions of the mind . . . Politics belongs to the domain of reason, but you mix it with religion. You pass into the other world of faith.' He complained that 'under this clause "as enunciated by Islam" you condemn us for ever to inferior status'. The Leader of the Congress, Mr. S. C. Chattopadhaya, protested even more vigorously. 'You are determined to create a Herrenvolk . . . This resolution in its present form epitomizes the spirit of reaction. That spirit will not remain confined to the precincts of this House. It will send its waves to the countryside as well . . .' For the minorities 'A thick curtain is drawn against all rays of hope, all prospects of an honourable life'.

Maulana Shabbir Osmani indeed may have given the non-Muslims some grounds for their apprehensions.

'The Islamic State', he said, 'means a state which is run on the exalted and excellent principles of Islam . . . People who do not subscribe to those ideas may have a place in the administrative machinery of the State, but they cannot be entrusted with the responsibility of framing the general policy of the State or dealing with matters vital to its safety and integrity.'

But the ministers who spoke for the Government emphatically repudiated the accusation that the privileges and status of the non-Muslims would be less than those of the Muslims. A non-Muslim, stated Liaquat Ali, could be at the head of the administration of an Islamic state. Non-Muslims, he said, would be

[1] The text of the resolution and of the speeches on it is taken from *Constituent Assembly of Pakistan Debates, Official Report, March 7th to March 12th*, 1949.

welcomed into the Government services of Pakistan, and the guarantees which were being given to them were much more comprehensive than those extended to the Muslims in the Dominion of India. The Foreign Minister, Sir Mohammad Zafrullah Khan, added that the minorities would be protected by the very teaching of Islam. 'It is a matter of great sorrow that, mainly through mistaken notions of zeal, the Muslims have during their period of decline earned for themselves an unenviable reputation for intolerance. But that is not the fault of Islam. Islam has from the beginning proclaimed and inculcated the widest tolerance. For instance, so far as freedom of conscience is concerned the Quran says "There shall be no compulsion" of faith.'

Iftikharuddin was the only Muslim critic of the resolution. He deplored its failure to guarantee political, social and economic justice. 'The fight in this country,' he said, 'is not going to be between Hindus and Muslims. The battle in times to come will be between Hindu have-nots and Muslim have-nots on the one hand, and Muslim and Hindu upper and middle classes on the other.'

He was answered by Sardar Abdur Rab Nishtar, Minister for Communications, who asserted that between capitalism and Communism Islamic democracy was a third way. 'If you are really serious in opposing capitalism as represented by certain countries of the West, and Communism as represented by Russia, then put forward an alternative social system. We, the Muslims, believe that a society based upon the Islamic principles of freedom, equality and social justice, to the Muslims and non-Muslims, believers, and non-believers, men and women, poor and rich, everybody, our own citizens and foreigners, can be the best alternative.' Liaquat Ali was equally emphatic. 'When we use the word democracy in the Islamic sense, it pervades all aspects of our life; it relates to our system of government and to our society with equal validity, because one of the greatest contributions of Islam has been the idea of the equality of all men.' Maulana Shabbir Osmani, perhaps the most learned

Islamic scholar in the House, explained that 'Islam has no truck with capitalism. The Islamic State brings about an equitable distribution of wealth by employing methods peculiar to it and distinct from communistic practices' and went on to describe those methods in detail.

Certain conclusions encouraging to liberals may be drawn from the debate. The men who are running Pakistan are determined to maintain it both as a social and political democracy. Although it is intended that Muslims shall be subject to the economic and social obligations prescribed by their religion, there is to be no distinction between Muslims and non-Muslims in the rights of citizenship. If the Hindus, still close to the horrors of 1947, are not yet convinced of the impartiality of their treatment, it is at least creditable that they feel able to voice their complaints freely. All parties are agreed on the necessity for a Judiciary independent of the Executive and the Legislature, and no one has suggested that it is not at present independent.

An interesting footnote to the debate was a resolution passed by the Christians.

'In our opinion', they said, 'the Objectives Resolution should set at rest the doubts which often assailed the non-Muslims of Pakistan with regard to the connotation of the term "Islamic State", which it was feared would be a theocratic state at variance with the democratic ideas of modern times.'[1]

After the Objectives Resolution had been passed, the Constituent Assembly appointed a committee of all parties 'to report on the main principles on which the Constitution of Pakistan is to be framed'. This committee has set up separate sub-committees to examine (*a*) fundamental rights, (*b*) franchise, (*c*) judiciary, (*d*) federal and provincial Constitutions. Until it reports little more can be known of Pakistan's future Constitution. Some trends, however, may be observed. Firstly, it seems universally agreed that both in the provinces and at the Centre every adult male will have a vote. Secondly, there is considerable,

---

[1] Resolution of the General Assembly of the All Pakistan Christian League, West Punjab, 5th April 1949.

though not general, support for a proposal to merge the three provinces of Western Pakistan, namely Sind, West Punjab and the North West Frontier Province, into a single unit of the Federation. Thirdly, some of the Constitution makers appear attracted by the separation of the executive and the legislature on the American model.[1]

[1] These observations are based on conversations which the writer has had with individual members of the Constituent and Provincial Assemblies.

CHAPTER VIII

Resources and Economy

Physical Features—Minerals—Agriculture—Industry
—Communications—Exports and Imports—Financial
Policy

The physical features of Western and Eastern Pakistan, separated from each other by 1,000 miles of Indian territory, are in marked contrast. Western Pakistan is bounded to the north and west by the Hindu Kush and Suleiman mountains, with peaks of 14,000 feet. These descend to the desert and plains of Sind and the West Punjab, whose sandy loam is watered by the Indus, Jhelum, Chenab, Ravi and Sutlej Rivers and by their extensive canal system. The rainfall is scanty and variable, averaging 9.4 inches a year in Karachi but 20.8 inches in Lahore. The temperature of the inland plains is extreme, varying between a maximum of 120 degrees in summer and a minimum of 28 degrees in winter nights. Eastern Pakistan on the other hand is largely a flat alluvial plain, through which the Ganges and Brahmaputra with their tributaries meander to the sea, covering the land with fertilizing silt during the rains. It has a tropical monsoon climate. The rainfall varies from about 75 inches in Dacca to 160 inches in Sylhet, and the temperature from between 45 degrees in winter to 102 degrees in summer. Western Pakistan, though far the larger area, has the smaller population. Its area is 306,920 square miles, with an average population density of 109 per square mile. Eastern Pakistan has an area of 54,015 square miles with a density of 850 per square mile.

The mineral resources of Pakistan, as at present exploited, are meagre and almost entirely in the west. About 500,000 tons of lignite coal are annually mined, but this is of poor quality and quite insufficient for the country's needs. West Punjab produces 15,000,000 gallons of petroleum oil per annum. The Burmah Oil Company is also prospecting in Sind with fair chances of success. Salt is exported from the West Punjab, and Sind manufactures cement from local limestone and clays. Baluchistan has large deposits of chromite which have only been lightly worked. Exploratory geological work is in progress.

The economy both of Western and Eastern Pakistan is therefore predominantly agricultural. In Western Pakistan 85.5 per cent and in Eastern Pakistan 95.2 per cent of the population live in villages. Eastern Pakistan is almost entirely rice eating, and although extensively cultivating rice, is not self-supporting. The diet of Western Pakistan is mostly wheat and other coarser food grains, though northern Sind both grows and consumes rice. Food statistics in the short and abnormal period since partition are not very reliable. It may be estimated that in an average year the rice surplus of Sind is not quite sufficient to cover the deficit of Eastern Pakistan, but that there should be a small exportable wheat surplus from Pakistan as a whole.

Pakistan has two cash crops which at present command excellent prices and on which, together with her self-sufficiency in food, her prosperity largely rests. East Pakistan grows about 70 per cent of the world's jute. Her annual exports of raw jute to India are valued at about £60,000,000, and to the rest of the world about £17,000,000.[1] West Pakistan's most important cash crop is cotton, 56 per cent of which is grown in the West Punjab and 28 per cent in Sind. In the year ending 31st March 1949, raw cotton to the value of £30,000,000 was exported by sea, in addition to a small quantity exported by land to India. In the same period hides and skins to the value of about £4,000,000 and raw

[1] Estimate of June 1949, before devaluation of the pound.

wool to the value of £2,500,000 were exported from Western Pakistan and tea valued at £2,800,000 from East Pakistan.

The rich agricultural lands of Western Pakistan are almost entirely dependent on artificial irrigation. Its canal system, radiating from and interlocking the Five Rivers, is the most extensive in the world. Thus 70 per cent of the crop area of the West Punjab and 77 per cent of the crop area of Sind are irrigated in contrast to only 8 per cent of the crop area of Eastern Pakistan. In the West Punjab, the Lower Chenab canal alone irrigates 3,000,000 acres. In Sind, the Sukkur barrage scheme, completed in 1932, irrigates 6,000,000 acres of land, whose annual rainfall averages less than 3 inches. As each new area was brought under cultivation in the nineteenth and early twentieth century, canal colonies were established whose cultivators, pioneers and re-settled soldiers were among the hardiest and best in India. Partition and the consequent transfer of populations affected the agricultural economy of Western Pakistan severely. The great irrigation system was divided, several of the most vital canal headworks being left in India and in Kashmir. The departing Sikhs were among the best cultivators in the canal colonies, and they took a large part of the livestock with them. They were replaced by more numerous, less efficient refugees with poorer beasts or none, and many of the landholdings had to be sub-divided.

These factors caused the wheat harvests of the West Punjab to be below average in 1947–8 and 1948–9. But in Western Pakistan, nevertheless, the future seems secure. Though there has been sudden pressure on existing landholdings, huge areas are still available for irrigation, and the Lower Sind Barrage, which should be completed in 1953–4, is alone expected to bring a further 2,700,000 acres under cultivation. The food situation in Eastern Pakistan is more serious, for there little cultivable land remains which is not already under rice or jute. In the famine of 1943–4, 1,500,000 Bengalis died, and the memory is one which cannot be forgotten either by the Pakistan or Provincial Governments. The population of East Pakistan, which was about 46,700,000 in 1948, will rise to about 55,000,000 by 1960, and the rice deficit will increase correspondingly unless agricultural methods become more intensive.

Both in Western and Eastern Pakistan mechanized cultivation is almost unknown. Cattle and buffaloes are the most important plough and draught animals. Camels are used extensively in Sind and sheep are grazed in the North West Frontier Province. Great quantities and varieties of fruit are grown: plums, pears, peaches, oranges and lemons in the west; tropical fruit such as pineapples, mangoes and bananas in the east. Broken communications with India have lost a valuable market, and fruit canning for export may provide alternative outlets. Both off the Sind coast and in the Bay of Bengal fish are plentiful and eaten locally, but lack of refrigeration prevents sea fish from being a staple article of the Pakistani diet inland.

The British East India Company first became established at the seaports, and it was round these, particularly Calcutta and Bombay, that Indian industry developed. The Indian Muslims were backward in industry and commerce, and even when factories were started inland they were concentrated in Hindu areas. Thus at Partition, Pakistan, though the world's greatest jute grower, had no jute mills, and of her annual production of 1,500,000 bales of cotton only 160,000 bales were consumed by her own cotton mills. Similarly, her hides and skins, wool, sugar-cane and tobacco all had to be sent to India or abroad for manufacture. She was entirely dependent on imports for armaments, having no ordnance factories. Consequently Pakistan, while free from India's handicap of a heavy food deficit, is faced with a far greater problem of industrialization, rendered more urgent by her embittered relationship with India.

The Pakistan Government has from the beginning appreciated this urgency and has amended the Government of India Act in order to subject key industries to central, instead of provincial, planning. In two statements of industrial policy issued in April and September 1948,[1] it declared that:

[1] Published by Industries Ministry, Karachi, 1948. Also in *Pakistan*, British Industries Fair Review, London, 1949.

Resources and Economy

1. The following industries were to be owned and operated by the State:

(a) Arms and munitions of war
(b) Generation of hydro-electric power
(c) Manufacture of railway wagons, telephones, telegraph and wireless apparatus.

2. The following industries were to be subject to central planning:

1. Arms and munitions of war
2. Cement and cement products
3. Edible oil, hydrogenated or otherwise
4. Electrical communications and broadcasting
5. Electricity, including hydro-electric power
6. Electrical equipment, appliances and goods
7. Glass and ceramics
8. Heavy chemicals
9. Iron and steel
10. Machine-tools, precision-tools, gauges and workshop equipment
11. Manufactures of heavy engineering industry
12. Minerals, including salt and coal
13. Non-ferrous metals and alloy manufactures
14. Paper, cardboard and pulp
15. Petroleum and mineral oils
16. Pharmaceuticals, drugs and light chemicals
17. Power and industrial alcohol
18. Preserved and prepared foods
19. Products of carbonization industry
20. Rubber manufactures
21. Scientific and mathematical instruments
22. Sea fish and its products
23. Ships, barges, river boats and lighters
24. Sugar
25. Tanned leather and leather goods

26. Textiles—cotton, woollen, jute, silk and rayon
27. Tobacco.

3. 'Pakistan would welcome foreign capital seeking investment from a purely industrial and economic objective and not
seeking any special privileges,' but participation of Pakistanis
must be ensured in administrative and technical services in the
industries concerned. Pakistanis should ordinarily be given the
option of subscribing at least 51 per cent of the shares of thirteen
named industries, and at least 30 per cent of the shares of other
industries.

The industrial progress of Pakistan depends mainly on four
factors: capital, technical skill, power, and communications.

To encourage capital, the budget of 1948 announced that new
industries using power machinery and employing more than
fifty men would during the first five years be exempt from income tax, super tax and business profits tax on any profits not
exceeding 5 per cent. Nevertheless the results have been somewhat disappointing. Pakistanis have preferred to invest their
money in commerce, where in a time of expansion, particularly
in Karachi, profits have been more rapid and certain than in
industry. Foreigners, though convinced by now of the stability
of Pakistan's economy, have been shy of making heavy invest-
ments while the Kashmir dispute, which has sometimes verged
on war, remains unsettled. They have also complained of an
income tax which is higher than that in India, of accommodation
difficulties in Karachi, and of severe delays at the Chittagong
docks. With the expansion of Greater Karachi, however, and
the development of the port of Chittagong, these latter difficulties will be removed. If Pakistan could settle her differences
with India, foreign capital would almost certainly come steadily
in. For by Eastern and Middle Eastern standards, the Pakistan
Government is efficient and well disposed to the West. Local
capital may be induced into industry by making the grant of
export and import permits dependent on investment in development schemes.

110

Resources and Economy

The shortage of technicians is regarded by the Finance Minister, who is also Minister for Economic Affairs, as more serious than the need for capital. Pakistanis are being trained in England, America and France. In the meantime, a remarkable variety of foreign experts can be seen in Karachi. The consulting engineers to the Government are a combination of two Swedish and one British company. A British company is responsible for aircraft maintenance. British, Australian and American pilots work for the civil airlines; Germans are employed in the chemical industries.[1]

For motive power, Pakistan must depend on the expansion of its water resources until its production of coal and oil is substantially increased. Under a six-year plan now in operation, the total electrical energy of the country is to be trebled. In Eastern Pakistan, the Karnafulli river, on which Chittagong is situated, is being harnessed to generate 60,000,000 kilowatts, primarily to provide power for the new jute mills. The Rasul project on the Upper Jhelum Canal will benefit about thirty towns in the West Punjab and will also extend irrigation. The Mianwali scheme, on the Indus, will develop a backward part of the West Punjab. Perhaps politically most important are the projects in the North West Frontier Province, at Malakand and Warsak, which have the dual purpose of making the province self-sufficient in food and, by supplying power to marble, coal, gypsum and copper mines and to cottage industries, to raise employment in the tribal areas.

Pakistan's communications have the defects natural to her position as the successor to political authority in two separate areas of a much larger empire. She has two main railway systems, the North Western broad gauge in the west and the East Bengal metre gauge system in the east, with a total of 6,994 miles. Much of the North Western Railway has been built for strategic rather than commercial purposes, and it was not self-supporting

[1] In December 1949 Displaced Persons from Latvia, Hungary, Yugoslavia and Russia, mostly doctors, dentists and teachers, arrived in Karachi under the auspices of the International Refugee Organization.

at Partition. On both railways, but particularly on the East Bengal Railway, locomotives and coaches had been worn out during the war. The rolling stock is being slowly replaced, though deliveries of locomotives from abroad have been slow. The North Western Railway is now paying it way.

The metalled road system of Western Pakistan was, for strategic reasons, better than that in many parts of India. It has, however, suffered severely from wartime use and from the refugee convoys. In Eastern Pakistan metalled roads hardly exist. The rivers are the main lines of communication, and the bullock cart and lorry of Western Pakistan are paralleled by the sailing boat and steamer.

The passenger-train service between West and East Punjab has not been resumed since the ambushes of 1947. At present it is only possible to travel from Karachi to Dacca by rail through Jodhpur, where a gap of seven miles has to be traversed by camel. Sea and air are therefore the normal links between Western and Eastern Pakistan. Western Pakistan has an excellent port in Karachi, with twenty-one wharf berths and a daily handling capacity of 12,000 tons of cargo. East Pakistan has a good natural harbour at Chittagong. This has in the past been neglected in favour of Calcutta, and has only four berths with a capacity of discharging less than 2,000 tons a day.[1] The expansion of Chittagong's port facilities, which is now planned, is vital not only for the development of an indigenous jute industry, but in order to enable rice to be sent from Sind to lessen East Bengal's regular deficit.

Whereas the sea voyage from Karachi to Chittagong takes nearly two weeks, a regular Pakistani civil air service takes passengers from Karachi to Dacca in between seven and ten hours. Lahore, Rawalpindi, Peshawar and Quetta are also linked to Karachi and Dacca by the two locally owned lines, Orient Airways and Pakair, flying Dakota and Convair machines.

[1] In October 1949 it was reported that two additional temporary berths had been constructed at Chittagong and that an American expert had been appointed as Chairman of the Port.

Resources and Economy

Pakistan has no international line of its own, but most of the principal foreign airlines pass through Karachi, which is one of the best and longest established aeroplane and seaplane bases in Asia.

In spite of the initial disadvantages, industrial progress is being made. The Pakistan Government is setting up three jute mills, which may later be sold to private ownership, and two other mills are being built privately. By the end of 1949 five new cotton textile mills are scheduled to be in production and two woollen and worsted mills completed. By the end of 1950 the 1947 output of the textile industry is to be trebled. The Mardan sugar factory, now under construction, will have an annual output of 50,000 tons. The factories of Sind already produce nearly 600,000 tons of cement a year. Progress has been slower in the industries needing technical skill; engineering, which was severely affected by the loss of Hindu skilled labour, ordnance, and the chemical factories which it is proposed to link to it. Sind is perhaps going ahead faster than other parts of Pakistan. Not only does it encircle the federal capital and greatest port, but its Government sponsors an admirable Industrial Trading Estate. This is a government-financed, non-profit-making public company owning industrial sites in Karachi, Hyderabad and Sukkur which are leased to individual industries. The company provides water, electricity and other services and is also prepared to construct factories for tenants who may not be familiar with local labour conditions.

The Muslims had very little share in the banking of undivided India, and even in 1949, out of the thirty-five principal banks operating in Pakistan, only two had their headquarters within the Dominion. The establishment of the State Bank, however, in July 1948, confirmed Pakistan's fiscal autonomy. The State Bank is both banker to the Central and Provincial Governments and is also a shareholders' bank. It controls and regulates the currency, credit and foreign exchange of Pakistan, which has had its own notes and coinage since 1948. 49 per cent of the shares in the bank are held by the general public. Three of the eight directors are elected by the shareholders; the remainder and the

Governor are nominated by the Government. The State Bank, in addition to its other functions, is training a hundred young Pakistanis for the banking profession.

Pakistan is a member of the sterling area. During the war of 1939–45 India was a great supply base for the British forces in the Middle and Far East. As a result the United Kingdom incurred a considerable debt to the Government of India, and Pakistan at Partition acquired a $17\frac{1}{2}$ per cent share of this credit, generally known as the 'sterling balances'. Pakistan's expenditure of her sterling balances is regulated by annual agreements with Britain.

For the first two years of independence, the currency exchange position was straightforward. The Pakistan rupee was freely interchangeable at par with the Indian rupee, and retained the old exchange rate of 13.2 rupees to the English pound, and 3.2 rupees to the U.S. dollar. In September 1949, however, the English pound was devalued from a rate of 4.03 U.S. dollars to 2.80 U.S. dollars. India devalued its rupee to a similar extent. Pakistan took no action. Thus, whereas the Pakistan rupee retained its old dollar valuation, its new exchange rate, quoted in Karachi, was 9.26 Pakistan rupees to the pound, and 69.50 Pakistan rupees to 100 Indian rupees.[1]

Pakistan's decision not to devalue was explained in a broadcast by the Governor of the State Bank. 'Pakistan is a predominantly agricultural country, and is in need of industrialization. Devaluation would have placed the hard-currency area beyond its reach, which is a cheap and ready source of capital goods.'[2] He believed that the decision would lower the price of imported consumer goods and consequently bring about a fall in the cost of living, especially in East Bengal. On the other hand, Indian merchants at the end of September were refusing to buy Pakistan's jute and cotton at the new exchange rate, and the London *Economist*[3] predicted a flight of capital from Pakistan. It seemed

[1] *Statesman*, Weekly Edition, 24th September 1949.
[2] Broadcast from Karachi, 22nd September 1949. Text from Pakistan High Commissioner's Office, London.
[3] 1st October 1949.

114

Resources and Economy

clear that the rate could only be held if there was a simultaneous fall in food and other basic prices within the country.

The extent to which Pakistan can import both consumer goods and the machinery necessary for industrialization depends mainly on her capacity to export raw materials. In the first six months of her existence she retained the tight import controls which had been in force in British India, and her import machinery was dislocated by the flight of the non-Muslims who had maintained it. The result was that in the period 15th August 1947 to 31st March 1948, she had a highly favourable balance of trade.

Pakistan's Exports and Imports Valued in Lakhs[1] of Rupees,

15th August 1947–31st March 1948

Country	Exports	Principal Items	Imports	Principal Items	Balance
U.K.	13,16	Tea, cotton, jute, wool	472	Machinery, textiles, cycles	+ 844
U.S.A.	467	Jute, wool, cotton, hides	400	Machinery, oil, metals	+ 67
Total all countries[2]	42,06		13,88		+ 28,18

(Statistics from *Pakistan*, British Industries Fair Review, London, 1949.)

Import controls were then relaxed to allow greater quantities of textiles, machinery, chemicals and vehicles to come in. In the year July 1948 to June 1949 the balance of trade with Britain thus became unfavourable. Both the balance with the hard-currency area and the overall balance, however, remained favourable.

[1] A lakh is 100,000. A lakh of rupees=approximately £7,619 sterling or U.S. $29,850, before devaluation.

[2] Exclusive of India, for which no figures are available.

Resources and Economy

Pakistan's Seaborne Exports and Imports, Valued in Lakhs of Rupees, July 1948–June 1949

Country	Exports	Imports	Balance
U.S.A.	11,62	11,50	+ 12
Total hard-currency areas	17,34	15,54	+ 180
U.K.	19,95	36,17	− 16,22
India (by sea only)	1,01, 87	40,90	+ 60,97
Total all countries	1,77,27	1,28,60	+ 48,67

(Statistics from Pakistan High Commissioner's Office Bulletin, 7th October 1949.)

The Pakistan Government's finances show a steady improvement over the past two years. At the time of Partition, the position was precarious. An interim budget, based on the assets and liabilities which had been taken over from the current Indian budget, showed a deficit of 234,000,000 rupees in the period August 1947 to March 1948. Moreover, India was reluctant to hand over Pakistan's share of the cash balances. To meet the emergency a loan was raised within Pakistan. This was enthusiastically oversubscribed, women even offering to pawn their jewellery to the Government. The budget for the year 1948–9 showed a slight surplus, however. In fact, the revised estimates at the end of the period proved it to be larger than expected. The budget for the current year 1949–50 anticipates another surplus, although expenditure has been considerably increased.

The two balanced budgets have owed their success to steadily increasing receipts from customs, excise, income tax and sales tax. In general, the Finance Minister has sought to benefit the poorer classes. In the current year the sales tax has been removed from essentials such as food grains, vegetables, milk and kerosene oil, and the lowest-paid government employees have received an increase in salary. On the other hand, import duty on luxuries such as tobacco, silk and gold and silver thread fabrics has been raised, and income tax and surtax are higher than in India. 43 per cent of the current expenditure is for defence. This is a lamentably high proportion, and directly relevant, as the Finance Minister hinted in his Budget speech, to Pakistan's differences with India. At the same time, it cannot fairly be compared with the proportionate expenditure in most other countries' budgets, since in Pakistan the provinces have their own budgets and sources of revenue to pay for the social services. The Central Government has, however, set aside for the year 1949–50, after meeting its own obligations of defence, railways and posts and telegraphs, 18.8 per cent of the budget for nation-building activities, mostly for public health and medical services. It also continues the subventions to the North West Frontier Province and to Baluchistan which were paid by the Government of undivided India.

CHAPTER IX

Western Pakistan

*The North West Frontier—West Punjab—Sind—
Baluchistan and the States*

THE NORTH WEST FRONTIER. The North West Frontier of
Pakistan consists of two distinct administrative units.
The settled districts, with a population in 1941 of about
3,000,000, form a province which is administered by a constitutional Governor, an elected Legislative Assembly and a responsible cabinet of ministers. The tribal areas and states, lying
between the province and Afghanistan, with a population in
1941 of 2,380,000, are governed by their own chiefs or councils
of elders under the supervision of the Agent of the Governor
General of Pakistan, exercised through various Political Agents.
The only constitutional link between the province and the tribal
areas is through the person of the Governor of the former, who
is also the Agent of the Governor General in the latter. The
privileged status of the tribes is a relic of British policy in the
expansionist era of the nineteenth century whose object was
always to have a 'buffer state' beyond its last acquired territory.
The rough boundary between the tribal areas forming part of
Pakistan and those coming under Afghan influence remains that
drawn by Colonel Durand in 1893. The Durand Line deliberately
avoided any contiguity between India and Russia. Thus, though
Pakistan has a six-hundred-mile border with Afghanistan, it
nowhere touches Soviet territory.

118

MAP OF
WEST PAKISTAN

Miles
0 50 100 150 200

Boundary
Provinces
Rivers
Railways
Cease-fire line
in Kashmir

Western Pakistan

The great majority of the inhabitants of the Frontier are Pathans, speaking Pushtu, which is also the language of Afghanistan, and having their origin in Afghanistan and Central Asia. The Pathan is tall, fair skinned and well built, and easily distinguishable by his dress—baggy trousers, velvet waistcoat and turban. He is strongly influenced by his zeal for Islam and by his love of liberty, but has a pleasant sense of humour. In the tribal areas he is bound by a primitive code of honour which obliges him to give sanctuary and hospitality to anyone who demands it, and to carry on blood feuds in retaliation for any insult to himself and his family. As a consequence, he is inseparable from his rifle and likes to build his house in the shape of a fort. The tribes are a martial, pastoral people, with poor agricultural land, prone to quarrel over grazing rights, and always tempted to raid the richer valleys of the settled districts. To maintain the peace, the British grouped them into five Agencies, in each of which the Political Agent held the individual tribes responsible for law and order in their own territory. Subsidies were paid to their maliks, or chiefs; and roads, schools and hospitals built. The Political Agent could enforce his authority by three methods. Firstly, each tribe had its own 'Khassadars' or police. If these proved inadequate, the agent could call on the Frontier Corps, an armed force about five thousand strong, recruited from the tribesmen, but paid by the Government and led by Indian police officers. Finally, strong detachments of the Indian Army were placed at strategic points within the tribal area and could be used to deal with major disturbances, such as those caused in recent years by the Fakir of Ipi. The province itself was defended from minor tribal raids by a Frontier Constabulary similar in organization to the Frontier Corps, but operating only within the settled districts.

There is no doubt that the presence of a foreign army, even though it was intended for defence against external as well as internal aggression, offended the Pathan at his two most sensitive points—his religion and his independence. Pakistan, believing that this had been the main cause of support for Ipi and

other leaders who had harassed the British, withdrew its army
entirely from the tribal area in December 1947, leaving their
defence to the Frontier Corps and other locally recruited scouts
and militia. The result so far has been satisfactory. All the tribal
chiefs or councils have acceded to Pakistan, and Jinnah, when
he visited Peshawar in April 1948, was enthusiastically greeted
by Maliks of the Afridi, Shinwari, Mohmand, Wazir, Mahsud
and Orakzai tribes. Each presented an address, and the points
made were very similar. They wished to maintain their direct
political relations with the Pakistan and not the Provincial
Government; they wanted more places in the armed and civil
services, and more schools, hospitals and factories. The representatives of Northern Waziristan also complained of the loss
of lucrative employment around military camps which had
followed the evacuation of the Army. Jinnah in his reply
promised that their subsidies would be continued and their
liberties retained. 'Pakistan', he added, 'wants to make you, as
far as it lies in our power, self-reliant and self-sufficient, and to
help your educational, social and economic uplift, and not to be
left, as you are, dependent on annual doles.'[1]

Another reason for the quietness of the tribal areas since
Partition has been the diversion of their interest and activity to
Kashmir. Although valuable plunder was probably taken in
Baramula and Mirpur, religious zeal was a more powerful
motive than loot in causing the tribal invasion of Kashmir. Long
after they were driven out of the Valley, their lashkars, regularly
reinforced and replaced, went on fighting against regular Indian
troops in the barren hills of Poonch, where nothing material was
to be gained. The representatives of North Waziristan told
Jinnah:

'May we respectfully but frankly tell you that it is impossible
for us to tolerate the repression and the systematic extermination of Muslims which is being carried out in Kashmir, and we
are determined to sacrifice our all to rescue our brethren from
the Dogra regime. We are sorry to say, however, that instead of

[1] *Frontier Information*, Peshawar, May 1948, pp. 11–16.

121

giving us help, Government has placed restrictions on our movements.'[1] What assistance they in fact received from the Provincial and Pakistan Governments has been bitterly disputed between India and Pakistan. Extracts from intelligence reports, published by the Pakistan Government, maintain that Pakistan officials worked hard to prevent the declaration of a 'jehad' (Holy War), and managed to postpone the invasion from August until late October 1947, by when the indignation of the Afghan as well as the Pakistan tribes could no longer be controlled.[2] It seems almost certain that they obtained transport, petrol and weapons on their way through the province, but whether those who assisted them acted on their own initiative or under instructions has never been proved. Abdul Quayum Khan, however, the Premier of the province, and himself a Kashmiri, made no secret of his sympathies. In his budget for 1949–50 he made special provision for resettling Mahsuds who had fought in Kashmir on lands within the province.

'The House will recall with pride,' he said, 'the fact that in our greatest hour of danger the Mahsuds responded to our call by rushing to the rescue of the oppressed Muslims of Jammu and Kashmir State, without any remuneration, and purely out of their sense of duty to protect the weak and oppressed. . . . The scheme of Mahsud colonization is but a humble token of appreciation of their wonderful services.'[3]

The tribesmen were withdrawn from Kashmir by the Pakistan Army after the Cease-Fire of January 1949, and their future is receiving considerable attention from the Pakistan and Provincial Governments. Their problems are economic and educational, and in both spheres progress in the tribal areas can only go forward in conjunction with that of the province itself.

Although the province in the referendum of July 1947 voted

[1] *Frontier Information*, Peshawar, May 1948, p. 12.
[2] *Intelligence Reports Concerning the Tribal Repercussions to the Events in the Punjab, Kashmir and India*, published by the Pakistan Government, Lahore, 1948.
[3] Budget speech of Premier, N.W.F.P., 7th March 1949, published by Government of N.W.F.P., Peshawar.

to join Pakistan, a Congress ministry, led by Dr. Khan Sahib, was still in office at Partition. The ministers took no part in the independence celebrations, and were dismissed by the Governor under instructions from Jinnah. A Muslim League ministry was then formed by Abdul Quayum Khan, and seven members of the Congress crossed the floor of the Assembly to support it. Elections throughout the previous ten years had shown Dr. Khan Sahib and his brother Abdul Ghaffar Khan, organizer of the 'Red Shirts', to have a clear majority over the Muslim League. But they appear now to have lost influence, as a result of refusing co-operation to Pakistan once it had been established, and for their courageous but personally inexpedient opposition to Pathan participation in the Kashmir war. Abdul Ghaffar has been detained in jail since June 1948, charged with conspiring against Pakistan with the Fakir of Ipi; Dr. Khan Sahib is confined to his village; and in May 1949 there were in all some three hundred and fifty political *détenus*.

Quayum, like one of his two colleagues in the Cabinet, is a former Congressman. In India he has aroused special hostility, partly as a 'renegade', partly as an 'organizer of the invasion of Kashmir'. In Pakistan, however, his influence, as holding firmly a delicate and strategic position, is considerable. In the Provincial Government he appears to have shown drive and imagination. 'The only way to increase our national wealth', he said in his 1949 budget speech, 'is by industrialization, by developing our trade, and by bringing more land under cultivation.' Progress towards all of these objectives depends largely on hydro-electric schemes which are now under construction. That at Warsak on the Kabul River is not only to generate between 100,000 and 200,000 kilowatts of electric power, but to bring 10,000 acres of land under cultivation in the Mohmand tribal area and in Peshawar District. The Dargai scheme and the extension of that at Malakand are to provide power both to the West Punjab and to the North West Frontier Province.

The province is heavily deficit in food grains, whose prices immediately after Partition were very high. Quayum believes that increased food production will follow drastic reforms in land tenure. He proposes therefore to abolish the permanent grants of 'jagirs' which have been made by previous governments to certain persons and their heirs for ever. Further, tenants-at-will are to become occupancy tenants after three years of continuous work and residence; and occupancy tenants are to acquire rights of ownership. These reforms have caused several landlords to leave the Muslim League and go into opposition in the Assembly.

Two of the districts of the province, Peshawar and Mardan, are fertile. In them the sugar crop has been doubled in the past ten years, and by irrigation and by reforms of land tenure, the production of wheat, which is the staple food, may be increased. But it is unlikely that the province as a whole, so largely mountainous, can ever be self-sufficient in food grains. On the other hand, nowhere in Pakistan are the raw materials for industry so varied, and the prospects of cheap electric power so good. One sugar factory is already producing 6,000 tons a year; another at Mardan, which will be completed in 1950, is expected to produce 50,000 tons of sugar a year; and it is possible that the North West Frontier Province may become capable of supplying most of Western Pakistan's sugar deficit. Fruit is abundant and cheap. A Government canning factory was built during the war, but has not so far proved able to compete with foreign canned fruit prices. Wool used to be exported to India, and there is now a need and an opportunity for local spindles and mills. Timber is plentiful, though reafforestation is necessary to repair wartime depradations, and the small match factory which is in production at Garhi Habibullah could profitably be expanded, as matches, which Pakistan previously obtained from India, are at present being imported from abroad. A tannery has been opened in 1949 at Nowshera, hides and skins being cheaply and plentifully available locally. Tobacco is grown in the province; it is all at present exported, but the Government hopes to set up a cigarette factory in 1950. The salt of Kohat has long been quarried as the cheapest in India. Marble, mica, and beryl are exploited to some degree, but the mineral resources of the province have not been adequately surveyed.

Raw materials, then, are abundantly available for development. The lack is of industrialists, technicians and office staff who may set up industries to exploit them. The Provincial Government is in no position to finance development schemes. It already receives an annual subvention of one crore of rupees from the Pakistan Government. The latter may advance funds from its Industrial Finance Corporation, but it cannot produce staff. In the long run the problem is therefore recognized as one of education. In the North West Frontier Province, in contrast to the West Punjab, the number of non-Muslims who left the province (269,000) far exceeded the number of Muslim refugees who came in (31,000), and the province suffered much more from the loss of trained and educated men than from the pressure of landless and homeless refugees. The Government has wisely started its educational reforms at the lowest rung of the ladder. The salaries of primary school teachers have been doubled, and in the course of three years the number of primary schools both in the province and the tribal areas is to be increased by 15 per cent.[1] A college of theology has been created, and its graduates, in addition to their religious duties, will be paid by the Government to organize adult literacy classes. At the higher level, a degree college for women, with both medical and general training facilities, has been budgeted, and the most ambitious project of all is to create a 'Khyber University' out of the various colleges in the province which are at present affiliated to the Punjab University.

The civil services of the North West Frontier Province were very seriously affected by the sudden departure of the Hindus. Hence the province has continued to depend more than others on British personnel. Sir George Cunningham, a former Governor who knew the tribes well and spoke Pushtu, was appointed

---

[1] Schools, hospitals, roads and other services in the tribal areas are financed by the Pakistan Government. The departments of the Provincial Government are, however, used to carry out the work.

the first Governor after Partition, and when his health broke down, he was replaced by Sir Ambrose Dundas, another officer well known on the Frontier. The Chief Secretary, Inspector General of Police, and Revenue Commissioner are still British. But the first Pakistani Governor, Colonel Khurshid, a Pathan, has now been installed, and it cannot be expected that the British will postpone their retirement from the administrative services much longer. On the other hand, the two leading educational institutions, the Islamia College and the Edwardes College, have British principals and assistants, and it is generally hoped in Peshawar that in this sphere, and especially in the proposed university, the British may continue to give help for many years to come.

Afghan propaganda has met with little success on the Frontier, and there are few signs of Communist activity. But the only way to confirm the loyalty and ensure the good behaviour of the tribes is by raising their standard of living. The initiative in this must come from the province. This is fully realized both by the Pakistan and Provincial Governments. The schemes are laid, and Quayum is energetic in pushing them forward. But no great advance can be made until the industrialists, technicians and administrators are available to carry them through. The training of such men cannot be undertaken in weeks or months; but there is an enthusiasm for education and for industrial progress which makes the long-range progress of the Frontier hopeful, unless external political factors intervene.

WEST PUNJAB. The Punjab was from the time of its annexation from the Sikhs in 1849 the favourite province of the British. The Lawrences, Edwardes, and its other administrators in the middle years of the nineteenth century were among the best in the British service, and their work was rewarded when the Punjab's loyalty enabled Nicolson to storm Delhi and check the Mutiny of 1857. In the later years of the nineteenth century the disadvantages as well as the benefits of British rule became obvious. The peasant found that though his rights in the land were now established, he had exchanged the tyranny of the Government for that of the moneylender; and the indefatigable legislators in the Viceroy's Council produced a spate of incomprehensible legislation which enabled the lawyer to absorb much of what the moneylender left. Yet in the twentieth century, the Punjab had the healthiest class of peasant proprietors in India; it provided the backbone of the Indian Army in both world wars; its canal system made it the richest agricultural province, and its co-operative societies, the best developed in the country, at least gave the enterprising peasant an opportunity of solvency. Its excellent university, founded in 1880, contained much of the finest in Hindu, Muslim, Sikh and Christian culture. Its capital of Lahore, proudly claiming the title of the 'Paris of India', was in winter the centre of a gay and cosmopolitan society.

Although the Muslims had a majority of the province's population, the Constitution of 1935 did not give them an absolute majority in the Legislative Assembly. Thus from 1937 to 1947 the Punjab had a coalition 'Unionist' ministry, led successively by Sir Sikander Hayat Khan and Khizr Hayat Khan Tiwana, supported by Muslims, Hindus and Sikhs, and basing its policy on the rural, as opposed to the urban, interest. Sir Sikander managed to combine his leadership of the Unionist Party with membership of the Muslim League. His successor, Khizr, however, quarrelled with Jinnah; the great majority of the Muslims went into opposition, and he remained precariously balanced on Hindu and Sikh votes until the Muslim League Civil Disobedience campaign brought down the ministry in March 1947. When therefore the League formed a ministry in the West Punjab after Partition, with the Khan of Mamdot as Prime Minister, its ministers had little administrative experience, and it proved quite inadequate to deal with the calamities by which it was faced. Iftikharuddin, the Refugee Minister and left-wing representative, soon resigned as a protest against the Government's failure to divide up large estates among the refugees. Mumtaz Daultana, perhaps its ablest member, and Shaukat Hayat, Sir Sikander's son, resigned in 1948. Amidst widespread allegations of corruption and mismanagement, Daultana tabled a vote of no confidence in the ministry. At this point the Pakistan Government intervened. In January 1949 the Governor General directed the Governor of the West Punjab to dissolve the legislature and to hold new elections.

'Public life', said the Governor General, 'has been demoralized by corruption, and the discipline of the Services destroyed by intrigue. . . . The main cause is the failure of the members of the Legislative Assembly, elected in different circumstances, to rise to the greater responsibility which independence brings.'

The Governor, Sir Francis Mudie, a retired British officer of the Indian Civil Service, was placed by this instruction in an invidious and, as it proved, impossible position. In order to hold fresh elections new electoral rolls had to be compiled which would include the refugees. This process would take at least a year, and in the meantime, though he was responsible to the Pakistan Cabinet, in the province he could be made to appear as a foreign dictator. Mudie had probably been more responsible than any of his ministers for the emergency arrangements which were made to receive the refugees in 1947. He now showed equal energy in exposing the corruption both among politicians and civil servants which had arisen from their failure to resist great temptations in the allocation of land and property to refugees. Mamdot himself was made to face an enquiry. The Commissioner of Rawalpindi was suspended, and it was clear that no one was to be spared. The Governor thus united against himself not only those elements who genuinely resented 'foreign rule' but all those who feared prosecution. A bitter Press campaign was given substance by a resolution of the Provincial Muslim League demanding his recall, and in July 1949, in circumstances which have not been made public, he resigned. He was succeeded by Sirdar Abdur Rab Nishtar, a Pathan, who had been Communications Minister in the Pakistan Government.

Yet if it has been made clear that in the West Punjab the men did not prove equal to the problems, it must be admitted that those problems might have baffled the wisest of governments. The emergency arrangements to receive the refugees were indeed not ineffective. At one time 51,000 homeless people were arriving each day in Lahore and over 1,000,000 were living in camps. To-day there are no refugees in camps.[1] Approximately 4,000,000 have been settled or absorbed in rural and 1,500,000 in urban areas. The province's population has increased by nearly 2,000,000 from the exchange of populations. Its resources are considerable, but not limitless. It inherited the great canal colonies of Montgomery, Lyallpur and Shahpur, a large part of which was vacated by Sikhs. Here each refugee cultivator who was settled with his dependants received between five and eight acres. Much of the northern districts of the province, however, and particularly in Rawalpindi and Attock, consists of poor, rocky land, already over-populated, many of whose inhabitants are obliged to earn their living in the army or on merchant ships. In the western districts, Dera Ghazi Khan, Muzaffargarh and Mianwali, is perhaps found the most indifferent cultivation and greatest poverty of all. The refugee cultivator who was settled outside the canal colonies received more land, up to $12\frac{1}{2}$ acres, but there seems no doubt that there are many who must be hard pressed to earn their bread, and that the standard of living among the agricultural population as a whole must, in spite of high food grain and cotton prices, have deteriorated as a result of the suddenly increased pressure on the soil. This pressure is accentuated by waterlogging in the canal colonies. Water seep-ing through the canal beds causes 25,000 acres of land to go out of cultivation each year and adversely affects another 50,000 acres, either by choking the roots of the crops in the subsoil, or actually coming to the surface. Waterlogging is being combated by drainage canals and by electrical pumping, but the process is delayed rather than checked.

The brightest hopes for the agricultural refugee lie in the Thal irrigation scheme and the Lower Sind Barrage. The com-pletion of the former scheme, which was started before Partition, has been advanced to 1950. It is expected to irrigate from the

[1] Except refugees from Kashmir, who hope eventually to return to the State.

Indus about 1,500,000 acres in the poorest part of the Mianwali District of the West Punjab, and some refugees have already settled there in anticipation of its benefits. Whether Punjabi refugees will stay on in Sind, even if they are guaranteed as good rights of land tenure there, still remains to be seen. Hitherto they have been very reluctant to go there, and although under Government arrangements more than 200,000 refugees have moved to Sind in 1948, many are reported to have gone back to the West Punjab.

Although more cultivators own their land in the West Punjab than in any other province, 50 per cent of the agricultural land is still rented. The forthcoming elections are to be fought on the basis of adult suffrage, and it seems likely that the League, under pressure from Iftikharuddin on the Left and Daultana in the Centre, will adopt a programme of land reforms. It may advocate the breaking up of large estates, or the reduction from the present rate of 50 per cent of the share of his produce which the tenant pays to the landlord, or the conversion of that payment into cash, so that the cultivator obtains the benefit of the present high prices. But at any rate, most Punjab Leaguers appear to believe that it is no longer possible for the League to continue without an economic programme, simply as an association of all patriotic Muslims; and weight of numbers is likely to swing that programme in favour of the landless labourer and the refugee and away from the landlord.

The fate of the urban refugee is more obscure than that of the rural refugee, which can be traced from land records. The former may be employed, partly employed, living on casual labour or on charity. At Partition, the West Punjab obtained a great surplus of artisans in trades in which Muslims specialize—weavers, tailors, blacksmiths and shoemakers. On the other hand, of the industries which might absorb them, the shoe factories and the cotton mills of the Punjab were mostly in the east, and those industries which were in the west, such as engineering and chemicals, were disorganized by the loss of Hindu skilled labour or management. In November 1948, of a total of 2,473 factories in the province abandoned by Hindus and Sikhs, 675 were still not working. The largest chemical unit, that producing soda ash at Khewa, was closed for over a year. Even when factories owned by non-Muslims were handed over to Muslims, the temporary and uncertain nature of their tenure often made the latter careless. Thus when a check was made in November 1948 of the 64 cotton-ginning factories which had been allotted to refugees, it was found that 16 were so badly damaged as to be unworkable, or no longer existed. Certain of the existing industries have absorbed a few refugees, in sports goods manufacture at Sialkot, and fruit processing at Sarghoda for instance. But substantial industrial rehabilitation awaits the expansion of industry which is planned by the Centre, and in which, of cotton and woollen mills and leather manufacture in particular, West Punjab will obtain its share.

Perhaps the happiest aspect of the Province's sombre history since Partition has been the advance of the Co-operative societies. Before Partition, the main work of the Co-operative Department was to provide credit and banking facilities for the cultivator. At Partition it widely extended its functions, for the exodus of Hindu traders and moneylenders both removed its natural enemies and left wide gaps in the provincial economy which it could fill. The Co-operative banks stepped into the place of the joint stock and commercial banks which closed down. They financed commerce, made loans to refugees, and served as government treasuries. They undertook the purchase of the wheat, rice and cotton crops, and prevented prices dropping to ruinous levels. Co-operative societies, consisting largely of refugees, were formed to run 26 abandoned cotton-ginning mills. The flight of Hindu shopkeepers enabled co-operative stores to be opened in each district, which have had a healthy influence in checking black marketing. Co-operative multipurpose societies handle the entire cloth distribution and much of the distribution of sugar, seeds, and agricultural implements of the province. Among the refugees, experiments in co-operative farming are being made, and weavers have been formed into societies and settled at selected centres where the Co-operative Department both supplies them with raw materials and markets their products. Altogether about 2 crores of rupees (£1,500,000)[1] was lent to the Provincial Government by the Co-operative banks between August 1947 and April 1949.

Education in the West Punjab appears to have made a rapid recovery from the setback of 1947, when many of the most distinguished professors left the university, and colleges were requisitioned for refugee camps. Lahore University had far greater prestige than Dacca or Karachi, and refugees from the East Punjab (which supplied five thousand teachers), the United Provinces and Hyderabad filled the staff vacancies throughout the province. Progress towards 'nationalization' is cautious. The matriculation examination can be taken in Urdu, but the B.A. examination will continue to be in English until a far wider range of text-books has become available in Urdu.

The Mamdot ministry was supported by the religious leaders. It introduced Prohibition, and made the principles of the Shariat binding for Muslims in personal law and inheritance. It also made religious instruction for Muslims compulsory in schools. The position of women has improved. Feminist leaders such as Begum Shah Nawaz have insisted that under the laws of the Shariat women had established rights of inheritance and divorce. In the field of education, two female adult literacy schools are being provided for every three male schools. Primary schools are co-educational; and at the Lahore Women's College there were two hundred Muslim intermediate science students in 1949, as compared with twelve in 1947. During the riots there was a natural tendency for women to go into seclusion, but it is now generally agreed that more Muslim women are out of purdah in Lahore than ever before.

We are still too close to the dislocation of 1947 to estimate the degree of the West Punjab's recovery and the prospects of its progress. Lahore today has a melancholy look. Its great bazaars and emporia, its restaurants, where one once had the choice

[1] Before the devaluation of the pound in 1949.

of chicken prepared in twenty different ways, its gay hotels and clubs, have lost much with the departure of Hindu and Sikh society and enterprise; and in many of its streets can be seen the misery of the homeless refugee, from Kashmir as well as India. Yet the tomb of Jehangir, the Fort of Akbar and the Mosque of Aurungzeb still stand to remind one that this was formerly the capital of the Mogul Empire. Lahore remains a nursery of poets, the intellectual and cultural heart of Pakistan; and if the politics and economy of the West Punjab have fallen on evil days, the influence of the Punjabis in the Central Government is far greater than might be expected from their numbers.

SIND. What the Nile is to Egypt, the Indus is to Sind. East of the river lies the Thar desert and the salt waste of the Rann of Cutch. To the west are the barren Kirthar Hills. The average rainfall is only 8 inches, and the summer temperature rises in places to 120 degrees. The extent of cultivation and the size of the population has been, until the growth of Karachi port, almost entirely dependent on irrigation from the Indus, along which also run the railway, river and road communications from the Punjab to the sea.

Sind's history has been as much shaped by its connections with the Middle East as with India. The Persians in the reign of Darius passed up the Indus; the Greeks under Alexander came down it from the Punjab. The Arabs in the seventh century A.D. conquered, converted and settled there. Akbar brought Sind into the Mogul Empire, but on the collapse of the latter the Ameers of Sind became feudatories of the Afghan Empire, and remained so until 1843, when the province was annexed by the East India Company in the course of a war with Afghanistan. It was merged with Bombay and was only re-established as a separate administrative unit in 1936.

The population reflects the history. Pathan, Arab, Baluchi and even African stock have mixed with that of the original Sindhi inhabitants who were converted to Islam. The Sindhi is tall, dark and robust, kindly, but an inferior cultivator to the

Punjabi, and with a reputation for indolence which may be partly attributed to the harsh climate. Educationally he is backward, and has been dominated by the Hindu trader and moneylender and by his own religious leaders, or Pirs. In contrast to the Punjab, Sind is a land of large estates in which the cultivator's rights have been inadequately protected.

Sir Richard Burton, passing through Sind in the eighteenfifties, called it 'the Unhappy Valley'. It is impossible to overestimate the change which has been brought about since that time through irrigation. The Lloyd Barrage at Sukkur was completed in 1930. The total irrigated areas of the province rose by 37 per cent between 1931 and 1938. The production of cotton between 1931 and 1941 was trebled and that of wheat quintupled. The successful introduction of the American long staple cotton produced a cash crop which found a ready market and high prices abroad. So sudden was the boom that there was a shortage of labour which was filled both by Muslim and Hindu immigrants from Rajputana, Cutch and Gujarat. Between 1931 and 1941 the Hindu rural population increased by 15 per cent, the Muslim rural population by 14 per cent. In the same period the Hindu urban population rose by 40 per cent, the Muslim urban population by 9 per cent. Karachi, whose importance grew with the productivity of its hinterland, had a slight Hindu majority in 1941, although in the province as a whole Muslims were 71 per cent in a population of about 4,500,000. Even the Census Commissioner, most cautious of all prophets, ventured to write in 1941: 'It is not unreasonable to contemplate a time when Karachi, with a huge cotton-growing area at its back door, may compete successfully with Bombay and Ahmedabad.'

At the time of Partition there was a Muslim League ministry in Sind, but commerce, industry and banking were almost entirely in Hindu hands, and Sikhs filled many important technical positions. Until the arrival of Muslim refugees from outside the province there was little communal feeling, and the Hindus, having much to lose, remained longer in Sind than in the West Punjab. A violent outbreak occurred in Karachi in

January 1948, however, and after it the great majority of middle-class Hindus emigrated by sea to Bombay. Their loss was immediately felt in the import trade and in industry, but was steadily compensated by the influx of Muslim traders from Bombay and Kathiawar. Educated and moneyed Muslim refugees from all parts of India tended to make for the capital of Pakistan, and Sind's commerce, industry and administrative services seem now, in 1949, less handicapped by shortage of trained personnel than those of the other provinces. There are still approximately 250,000 Hindus in Sind, and there have been indications, at times when inter-Dominion relations have been improving, that many of those who left would like to return. The Provincial Government, however, hard pressed to find both land and jobs for Muslim refugees, has not encouraged the Hindus to return.

The political history of Sind since Partition has been unhappy. The first Prime Minister, M. A. Khuhro, was dismissed by the Governor on the orders of the Governor General for mal-administration. His successor, Pir Illahi Buksh, was disqualified from public life for electoral misconduct. The present Prime Minister, Yusuf Haroon, was aged only thirty-three when he took office, and was not a member of the Legislative Assembly. Yusuf Haroon is a wealthy and widely travelled businessman, who was Mayor of Karachi at the age of twenty-eight. He has a broader outlook than his predecessors, and is likely to foster the industrialization of the province which he has described as 'a paradise for the capitalist'.[1] The first Governor of Sind after Partition was Sir Ghulam Hidayatullah, a veteran Muslim Leaguer, who had done much to persuade the British to separate the province from Bombay. On his death in 1948 he was succeeded by Din Mohammad, a retired High Court judge of the Punjab.

One cause of friction between the Sind and Pakistan Governments has been the decision of the latter to take over the administration of Karachi. Precedents for this step could be found

[1] In an interview with the writer, May 1949.

135

in New Delhi, Washington and Canberra; in its local context it was more than justified by the instability of the Sind ministry. Karachi, which had a population of 386,000 in 1941, has now grown to over 1,000,000, of whom 475,000 are refugees; accommodation difficulties are consequently very great, even for the diplomatic corps, foreign industrialists and Government officials. Greater Karachi is being ambitiously planned to accommodate 3,000,000, and the work has been entrusted to Swedish and British engineers. Government buildings will be located on both sides of the river, inland from the present city. 1,500 acres are being granted free to refugees for housing and commercial sites, and further grants of lands have been made to building co-operatives to erect private accommodation.

Karachi today appears a temporary, sprawling, untidy capital, with no obvious centre. Its description by an American journalist as 'a one camel town' is a little unfair, for it has some fine public buildings, built in the boom years of the 'thirties, and on the establishment of the Provincial Government in 1936. It has certain natural advantages. Its excellent port is the export and import centre for the whole of Western Pakistan and Afghanistan, and it also gives Pakistan a window to the Middle East. Its airport, on the main intercontinental route, is said to handle more night traffic than any other in the world. Its climate is healthy, a sea breeze blowing through the summer months, and it has pleasant bathing and sailing facilities. Land is plentiful, for it is on the edge of a desert. The only limiting factors in its expansion seem to be the extension of the water supply, and the import of steel for building construction, which is otherwise well served by the local cement quarries. As capital of an agricultural country, perhaps a potential danger is its isolation, with sea on one side and desert on the other, from the villages in which 90 per cent of the Pakistanis live. It would be possible in Karachi for the bureaucrat or diplomat to forget the real Pakistan, as he could not in Lahore or Dacca, where the land is cultivated right up to the edges of the city.

Apart from the expansion of Karachi as the Federal capital,

the future prosperity of Sind, and its ability to absorb refugees are likely to rest mainly on three particular projects. Agricultural progress will depend on the Lower Sind Barrage and on the Sind Tenancy Bill of 1949; industrial progress on the Sind Industrial Trading Estate.

The Lower Sind Barrage across the Indus, south of the Lloyd Barrage, is expected to be completed in 1952 and to irrigate between 2,500,000 and 3,000,000 acres, of which 1,000,000 acres will be brought under cultivation for the first time. The Provincial Government is planning to introduce tractors, under government or co-operative ownership, into the new area, where it anticipates a shortage both of labour and cattle. A labour shortage would on first thought seem surprising, since West Pakistan has received a surplus population of 1,500,000 or 2,000,000 as a result of refugee movements. In Sind itself, however, excluding Karachi, the number of non-Muslims who left exceeded the number of Muslims who came in. Punjabi refugees have been very reluctant to go to Sind. Part of this reluctance is based on dislike of a strange country, language, and climate. But there has also been a solid enough reason hitherto in the different land systems of the Punjab and Sind. Whereas in the Punjab the best land has been owned by the cultivators themselves, Sind has remained feudal. 80 per cent of the land is held by big landlords; 10 per cent of it is held by jagirdars, whose ancestors received the land in perpetuity as a reward for services to the British a hundred years ago. Whereas in the Punjab the cultivator sells his produce direct in the market, in Sind he sells to the landlord at well below market rate. The landlord thus obtains the full benefit of the present high prices of food grains and cotton.

The Sind Legislative Assembly has at present under consideration the Sind Tenancy Bill 1949, which the Revenue Minister has described as 'the Magna Charta of the Haris' (cultivators). Under its provisions, the tenant who cultivates four acres for three years for the same landlord is to acquire hereditary rights, of which he cannot be dispossessed as long as he maintains the land satisfactorily. The tenant-at-will, who has not yet acquired those rights, is guaranteed a fixed proportion of the crop and is protected against forced labour. His rights and duties and those of the landlord are comprehensively listed, and joint tribunals of landlords and tenants, presided over by a government officer, are to be set up to hear disputes arising from the Act.

It may be hoped that this legislation will not only encourage Punjabi refugees to settle in Sind, but will give to the Sindhi himself a sense of economic independence which will make him a better cultivator and give him a more intelligent and successful control than hitherto over the political destinies of the province.

Mention has been made in Chapter VIII of the Sind Industrial Trading Estates, Ltd., a public company whose capital is subscribed by the Sind Government but whose board of directors includes non-officials as well as officials. The Estates are the first attempt at large-scale industrial planning in the subcontinent. Thus industries depending on imports and skilled labour are encouraged to open on the Karachi Estate. Those depending on local raw materials, such as cotton, hides and oil seeds, or needing plentiful water, are advised to go to Hyderabad or Sukkur, which are market centres for these products and where water is cheaper than at Karachi. At the time of Partition there were 60 applications for factory sites in the Estates. The number has now risen to 250. 50 per cent of the industries which have opened, or are under construction on the Karachi Estate, are foreign, the great majority of these being British, and they are as various as textiles, pharmaceuticals, engineering, motor assembly, hosiery, cigarette making and boot manufacture.

Sind's economic prospects then are bright. New land is coming under cultivation. The natural resources are rich, a wheat and rice surplus, an excellent long staple cotton, the hardy Red Sindhi cattle, abundant fishing all along the sea coast and, what may prove most important of all, prospects of oil. To Karachi have come the wealthier Muslim refugees, traders and industrialists, and foreign capitalists and technicians. In its clubs, hotels and cafés, the talk is of the future, not of the past as in Lahore. The problems are those of a young province, political and educational backwardness. The presence of the Federal capital should inspire progress in both spheres. The Sind University, young and non-residential, is already benefiting from the cosmopolitan atmosphere of Karachi. Compulsory primary education is slowly being extended into the districts, although co-operative societies, which provide the best method of adult rural education, are not intensively organized. There has been no outbreak of the criminal Hurs since the execution of the Pir of Pigaro in 1944, but at least one outlaw band still exists and has caused murders on trains. The political leadership of the province has been disappointing, but the Central Government has acted firmly and vigilantly in dismissing two Premiers. The best hope of cleaner and more efficient politics is provided by the emancipation of the cultivator from the landlord by the Sind Tenancy Act.

BALUCHISTAN AND THE STATES. Baluchistan, though larger in area than Sind, had at the time of the 1941 census a population of only 857,000, which was steadily decreasing through emigration to more prosperous areas. It is a land of barren mountains and desert, with a rainfall of only 5 inches a year in the plains and 10 inches in the mountains. In its few fertile valleys cultivation is dependent on natural irrigation from open and underground springs. 25,000 tons of wheat have to be imported into the province annually, which are paid for by the export of animals, fruit, wool and medicinal herbs. Many races have left their influence on the population. Greeks and Arabs passed through Baluchistan, and Afghans conquered and settled there. The indigenous Baluchi is somewhat shorter than his neighbours, wears his hair in long curls and is an expert horseman. 90 per cent of the population in 1941 was Muslim.

Administratively the province is divided into (*a*) districts directly administered by Pakistan; (*b*) the states of Kalat, Las Bela, Kharan, and Mekran, which have acceded to Pakistan; (*c*) agencies which were originally leased by the Khan of Kalat

139

to the British, and are now administered by Pakistan. The Agent of the Governor General of Pakistan at Quetta represents the Central Government in all three areas. The diversity of administration is due to the British reluctance to assume full responsibility in this wild and unproductive country. A measure of control became inevitable during the Afghan War of 1843, and the present arrangements, which were inherited by Pakistan at Partition, date from 1875 when constant disorders, particularly in Kalat, brought about British intervention.

Kalat, with a population of 250,000 and an area of 53,000 square miles, is the largest political unit in Baluchistan. Las Bela, Kharan and Mekran were former feudatories of the Khan of Kalat which asserted their independence at the end of the nineteenth century.

Of the remaining states of Pakistan, Khairpur (population 300,000) is geographically, and has for most of its history been administratively, part of Sind. It owes its separate existence to the aid furnished by its ruler to the British in the first Afghan War, when the other Amirs of Sind opposed the British forces. It has shared in the recent economic progress of Sind, and its ruler in 1949 introduced representative government.

Bahawalpur lies between the West Punjab and India, and has the largest population (1,341,000) of the Pakistan states. Its ruler is descended from the Abbasid Khalifs of Egypt, and like Khairpur it owes its independence to an alliance with the British against the Afghans. Though much of Bahawalpur is desert, it has greatly benefited from the irrigation schemes of the Punjab, and exports 50,000 tons of wheat a year.

There are also states on the North West Frontier, of which Chitral, Dir and Swat are the most important. Their relationship with Pakistan is conducted through the Agent of the Governor General in Peshawar, and their status only differs from that of the tribes of the Frontier insofar as their rulers have recognized hereditary rights. Since the end of 1947 Pakistan has extended its *de facto* authority in this region over the tribes and chieftains of Gilgit and a large part of Baltistan, who were formerly feudatories of the Maharajah of Kashmir. The most important of these are the Mirs of Hunza and of Nagar, who control an important route into Central Asia. Pakistan's control is exercised through a Political Agent at Gilgit.

Whereas in India the population of the states which have acceded comprises about 25 per cent of that of the whole Dominion, in Pakistan it represents only about 5 per cent of the total population, drawn from small units of little economic importance. As yet the Pakistan states have no representation in the Constituent Assembly. It seems natural to suppose that in the course of time the Baluchistan states will join the Advisory Council which has been set up in the directly administered districts to assist the Agent of the Governor-General. The Provincial Governments of Sind and West Punjab may be expected to exercise increasing influence in Khairpur and Bahawalpur respectively, as the popular demand for democratic institutions grows within those states. But on the North West Frontier, despite strong economic and administrative arguments in favour of a merger of the tribal areas and states with the province, the Pakistan Government is likely to have to proceed very cautiously in face of the strong pride of the individual tribes in their independence.

CHAPTER X

Eastern Pakistan[1]

A t Partition, the aspect of Pakistan which caused most scepticism among foreign observers was the viability of its eastern province, which had been created out of the eastern areas of Bengal and the Sylhet district of Assam. Separated by a thousand miles from Western Pakistan, over-populated and with no local industry, its commerce, administration and communications centralized in the great Indian port of Calcutta, with a different language, dress, diet and way of life from the western provinces, it was rumoured to be likely very soon to secede quietly from its unnatural union with Pakistan and merge once more with West Bengal as a unit of the Indian Dominion.

These rumours have stopped, and a glance at the history of Bengal will show how little basis there was for them. From 1200, when the first Turki invaders came, until 1757, when Clive defeated the Nawab Suraj-ud-Daulah at Plassey, Bengal was ruled by Muslim dynasties, whether Afghans, Moguls or independent kings, and their capitals, Gaur, Dacca, and Murshidabad, were Muslim cities. The British built a new capital, Calcutta, in the Hindu-majority area of West Bengal. Under their rule the Services, commerce and industry, insofar as they were not manned by the British themselves, were dominated by the Hindus. The

---

[1] 'Eastern Pakistan' and 'East Bengal' are synonymous terms, used interchangeably in the Pakistan Press and in ministerial speeches, and consequently in this book. The Government of the province, however, is still officially the Government of East Bengal.

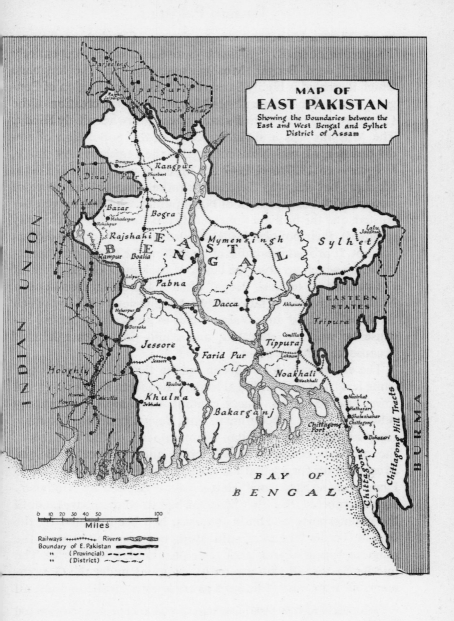

MAP OF
EAST PAKISTAN
Showing the Boundaries between the
East and West Bengal and Sylhet
District of Assam

huge Calcutta University was a preserve of Brahmin influence. The great modern Bengali literary movement was almost entirely Hindu; indeed Bengali Muslims maintain that the language which it created is highly Sanskritized. The contribution of Bengal to the Indian Independence Movement, to the creation of the Congress, and to modern Indian art was overwhelmingly Hindu. The Muslims had a slight majority in the population of undivided Bengal[1] which was reflected in the Legislative Assembly, and between 1937 and 1947 the ministry was always led by a Muslim; but this was the shadow rather than the substance of power. With the exception of Nazimuddin, who was universally trusted, and the brilliant Suhrawardy (and these two were openly opposed), their political leadership was generally dull and often corrupt. It proved incapable of abolishing the Permanent Settlement, by which an absentee landlord took most of the profit of the cultivator; in East Bengal often a Hindu landlord and a Muslim cultivator. It failed to break the vicious circle by which the Muslim could not obtain a place in government service because he was not educated; and could not educate himself because he was too poor.

The enthusiasm for Pakistan among the Muslims of Bengal came less from their political leaders than from the working and lower middle classes. Dacca contains more mosques than any other city in the subcontinent. East Bengal had been the most receptive soil for the puritan Islamic revival of the Wahabis in the previous century. The illiterate and uneducated Bengal Muslim never forgot that his ancestors had become converts to Islam because they came from a class oppressed by Hinduism. He remembered, too, that Muslims had ruled the province until the counterpoise of Hindu influence had been created by the British. To the labourers, cultivators, boatmen and artisans the religious appeal of an Islamic state was simple and effective. The middle classes, all who aspired to positions under the Government, all who wanted licences to trade in controlled goods, all

[1] Muslims were 33,000,000 out of the province's population of 60,000,000 in 1941.

who hoped to win scholarships, to teach, or practice at the Bar, saw Pakistan as a state in which the way to advancement would no longer be blocked by the wealthier and better educated Hindu.

They did not forget, when they agitated stridently for Pakistan in the 'forties, that from 1905 to 1912 East Bengal had been constituted as a separate province, and that the superior political organization of the Hindus had persuaded the British to annul the Bengal partition.

Dacca is a city of bamboo and corrugated iron, whereas Calcutta is proverbially a city of palaces. But the Muslim, still a little unsure of himself, preferred the homely atmosphere of the former, in the heart of a Muslim area, with a small university in which Muslims were at no disadvantage, to the splendour of the latter, where neither the presence of Muslim ministers nor of communal ratios ever convinced him that he received a square deal. The precise relation between East Pakistan and the Central Government has not yet been established. On many points, particularly over the delay in the development of the port of Chittagong, the former has been critical of the latter, and will probably continue to be so. But of any willing merger with West Bengal or India there seems no prospect. In education, commerce, industry, in the development of Dacca and Chittagong, in all branches of government service, the Muslims of East Bengal have seized opportunities which could never have come to them in united Bengal and which they are most unlikely ever willingly to relinquish.

In this the 32,000,000 Muslims of the province seem unanimous, but there is also in East Bengal, alone of Pakistan's provinces, a substantial Hindu minority. Probably about 12,000,000 remain, though over 1,000,000, including a high proportion of teachers and government servants, are said by India to have migrated to West Bengal. A particularly sensitive people, justifiably proud of their great contribution to Indian literature, art and politics, the Hindus of East Bengal bitterly resent their loss of influence. They have no representatives in the Cabinet, and though 30 per cent of the places in the Services are reserved for

K

non-Muslims, whether because candidates are shy or because there is a prejudice against them, the quota does not appear to be filled. Their tribulations have been slight by comparison with those of the Hindus of Western Pakistan. They still dominate the Dacca Bar and occupy one third of the places at the university. Their temple bells can be heard in the evening, and in their shops in the bazaar are exhibited portraits of Nehru, Patel and other Indian leaders. Their worst complaint is of the ruthless requisitioning of their houses. Their worst fear is of persecution not arising from a local cause, but from one of those violent inter-Dominion broadsides which are regularly fired by Indian and Pakistan ministers in the course of the Kashmir dispute. In the Provincial Legislative Assembly, Caste Hindus occupy 28 seats and Scheduled Castes 18 seats in a house of 171. The only hope of winning the whole-hearted loyalty of this substantial minority is by giving it representation in the Cabinet, which will also lead to its representation in the Services. The present Muslim League provincial ministers are aware of the importance of this step, but feel unable to make it while inter-Dominion relations remain strained almost to breaking point, and while Hindus and Congressmen can hardly fail to be suspected of sympathy with India. In the meantime the minority accepts its position not without dignity. 'Perhaps in the end,' said one of its leaders to the writer, 'though we have lost our political influence, we shall exercise the same civilizing influence on the Muslims as the Greeks did on the Romans.'

Somewhat unexpectedly, in view of past feuds among local Muslim leaders, the Muslim League ministry in East Bengal has proved more stable than those of Western Pakistan. Nazimuddin, who had been Premier of undivided Bengal from 1943 to 1945, and who is a relation of the Nawab of Dacca, became the first Prime Minister of the new province. His reasonable spirit permeated the administration and did much to prevent communal violence in the critical days of Partition. On his departure to Karachi in 1948 to become Governor General of Pakistan, he was succeeded by Nurul Amin, a quiet but well-liked barrister

Eastern Pakistan

who had been Speaker of the Legislative Assembly of united Bengal. Perhaps the most energetic of the ministers has been Hamidul Huq Chowdhury, Minister of Finance, Commerce, Labour and Industries, but the Cabinet as a whole has been more concerned with the emergency work of setting up a new capital and administration, and with holding off a food crisis and inflation, than with any spectacular reforms.

The economic problems of East Bengal are characteristic of the tropical areas of South East Asia. Rice grows plentifully in the fertile silt of the Ganges and Brahmaputra rivers, but not abundantly enough to match the increase in population, which in united Bengal grew from 50,000,000 in 1931 to 60,000,000 in 1941, and which, together with wartime transport difficulties, preventing an import of rice from outside, caused the appalling famine of 1943–4, with a death-roll officially estimated at 1,500,000. The southern districts of East Bengal, deltas and islands, with no railways and few roads, suffered worst of all in the famine, and since Partition the price of rice has again from time to time risen dangerously high in the area. Imports from Western Pakistan have so far enabled the Provincial Government to flood the markets and at least keep prices below famine level, but the process will become increasingly difficult as the population grows. The Pakistan Food Ministry estimates that, unless local production is intensified, by 1954 East Bengal will have to import 5,000,000 tons of foodgrains a year, and by 1959, 10,000,000 tons. In contrast to Western Pakistan, relatively little waste land can be brought under cultivation. On the other hand, productivity per acre is low, less than half that of Japan, for example. The need, therefore, is to increase the yield by modern agricultural methods, to draw off into industry the surplus agricultural population, and to give the agriculturalist and his family subsidiary work in cottage industries in the long periods of idleness on the land. The high price of rice is related to the high price of jute, and the shortage of consumer goods in the province. Pakistan produces about three-quarters of the world's raw jute, whose cultivation is strictly controlled by the Provincial

147

Government in order to maintain the price. In the post-war 'seller's market' this has remained high, dangerously high perhaps by comparison with that of the jute substitutes which are being evolved in America. It cannot, however, be reduced unless the price of rice, which is the basic food of the jute grower, falls first. The flow of consumer goods which formerly came in through Calcutta was suddenly diminished at Partition, and the port facilities at Chittagong could not be expanded rapidly enough to bring in goods by an alternative route. This shortage has contributed to the general inflation.

Ironically, an important factor in the growth of the population and consequent danger of famine has been the advance of medical science. It was estimated that in united Bengal in the decade before the famine of 1943, 400,000 deaths occurred annually from malaria. The wide and cheap distribution of paludrine and other drugs reduced the rate by 1947 to 150,000.[1]

On the other hand, the inertia caused by frequent bouts of malaria has been a factor in the low productivity and lack of enterprise of the cultivator; if this is lessened by anti-malarial drugs, he may become more responsive to new agricultural methods and to part-time or whole-time industrial employment.

Yet one of the most fundamental causes of the poverty of Bengal and of its agricultural backwardness is not attributable to nature but to the benevolent gesture of a British Government. It is said that Pitt, when Prime Minister of England, shut himself up with the files for ten days in his house at Wimbledon before approving the Permanent Land Settlement of Bengal which was promulgated by Lord Cornwallis in 1793.[2] Seldom can such administrative zeal have been so misapplied. Pitt and Cornwallis acted with admirable generosity in forswearing for the duration of English rule any increase in the rate of land revenue which should be paid to the East India Company as the government of the territory. They hoped thereby to increase the

[1] Information from East Bengal Government, Public Health Department.
[2] O'Malley, *History of Bengal*, p. 260.

security, productivity and prosperity of the landed interests. But they vested in the 'zemindar', who had been a tax farmer with no established hereditary rights under the Moguls, the privileges and authority of an English eighteenth-century landlord. Although the rent which was payable by the zemindar to the Company was fixed, the amount which he could demand from the tenant was unlimited. Many years later, the position of the latter was to some extent safeguarded by the Bengal Tenancy Act of 1885. But until the end of British rule, despite the recommendations of the Floud Commission and the resolutions of successive Provincial Governments, the land revenue of Bengal was ludicrously limited to that payable in 1793, and the beneficiary from this light assessment was not the cultivator, but a class of hereditary landlords, few of whom resided on their estates.[1]

The present East Bengal Government is committed to the acquisition of the zemindaries by the state. This is bound to be a long and complicated process, and the substantial funds for the compensation of the landlords can only come from a loan from the Centre. Survey work is, however, being carried out to enable the necessary legislation to be prepared.

Although East Bengal contains two-thirds of the population of united Bengal, it inherited only 12 per cent of the industrial installations of the province, which were concentrated around Calcutta and in the iron and coal area of the Bihar border. One result of this industrial backwardness, together with the poverty of the cultivator and the shortage of consumer goods, is that only Rs. 4/8 per head is raised annually by provincial taxes, as compared with Rs. 17/8 in West Bengal, Rs. 18/9 in Sind and Rs. 7/9 in West Punjab.[2] Financially the province is engaged in a double struggle, with West Bengal for various assets which are still considered due from the Partition settlement, and with the Pakistan Government, which not only obtains that share of the

[1] The Floud Report (Calcutta, 1940), vol. i, chapter ii, summarizes the consequences of the Permanent Settlement.

[2] Budget speech of Finance Minister, East Bengal, 1949. Published by East Bengal Government, Dacca.

export duty on jute which was formerly taken by the Government of India, but has also appropriated the entire proceeds of the income tax and sales tax. East Bengal's capital expenditure on its new administrative buildings and staff quarters, and on the expansion of the hospital and university at Dacca, has been unavoidable and considerable. It has ingeniously saved money, however, by recovering the entire cost of the enormous Civil Supplies Department, which procures and distributes food and rationed articles, from the sales price of the commodities in which it deals. Through this saving in the current budget the Government has been able to set aside 1 crore of rupees (£760,000 in June 1949) for industrial development.

Industrialization is vital for the province, in order to find employment for its surplus labour, to increase its revenues, and to decrease its economic dependence on Calcutta. The most obvious opening is for jute mills, of which there were none in the province at the time of Partition. The West Bengal Government has, however, been unwilling to allow the transfer of milling equipment from Calcutta; and both Pakistani capital, which is mainly concentrated in the West, and foreign capital, which has a strong vested interest in Calcutta, have been shy of investment in new mills. Nor is this altogether surprising, while Chittagong port remains a bottle-neck, and while Dacca contains no modern facilities. The East Bengal Government hopes to 'prime the pump' by establishing two jute mills, two cotton mills and one paper mill, with allied chemical plants.[1] The public will be invited to take up shares in them, but the unsubscribed capital will be guaranteed by the Government. The pace of industrialization is limited by the availability of power, and much depends on the Karnafulli hydro-electric scheme at Chittagong which has been initiated since Partition. Lack of technicians, skilled labour, and efficient office staff are further handicaps to industry. There is an engineering college at Dacca, and technical students are sent abroad for training at Government expense. The establish-

[1] These are in addition to the mills financed by the Central Government, and referred to in Chapter VIII above.

ment of Institutes of Ceramics, Tanning and Textiles was also provided for in the 1948 and 1949 budgets, but all branches of education lost ground at Partition from the exodus of Hindus, and in the sudden dislocation from Calcutta. The Dacca University, founded in 1921, was before Partition small and residential. The remaining colleges throughout the province were affiliated to the Calcutta University. At Partition, those colleges which were in East Bengal were affiliated to Dacca, which, at a time when its staff was severely depleted by the loss of Hindus, suddenly had to increase its examining and degree-giving functions. The university has sought, not entirely successfully, to obtain British and European professors and lecturers to fill some of the vacancies.

Students in Bengal have traditionally played an active part in politics, campaigning in elections and doing social work in the villages. Since Partition, they have been vociferous, even at times tumultuous, in Dacca, and on one occasion confined the Vice-Chancellor and Senate in the Council Room. Their discontent was concentrated early in 1948 on the language question, when it was alleged that the Central or Provincial Government intended to replace Bengali by Urdu. Jinnah, addressing the University Convocation in March 1948, made it clear that although Urdu was to be the official language of Pakistan, the province was free to make Bengali the provincial language if it wished, and hinted that the language controversy had been fomented by the Indian Press, and by 'fifth columnists'.[1]

Whether, as is sometimes stated, Communism has been mainly responsible for student discontent is doubtful. It is true that no province of Pakistan is more open to Communist influence. For though East Bengal has itself a very small industrial population, on the one side West Bengal has for many years been a Communist centre, and on the other lies the chaos of Burma; it is easy for agents to cross either border. Moreover, in the famine of 1943 Communist and Communist-influenced relief organizations carried out energetic relief work in the southern districts,

[1] Speech to Dacca University Convocation, 24th March 1948. *Speeches as Governor General*, p. 66.

which might again ensure them a favourable reception from the artisan and landless labourer if food prices were to remain high. There may, too, be wide support for opposition to the existing government among all classes of Hindus, so long as they are excluded from political influence. But in the immediate future organized opposition to the present ministry is more likely to be concentrated round the leadership of Suhrawardy, who once had, and probably still has, a strong following among left-wing elements within the League. Since his migration from India to Pakistan, one of his supporters has defeated a government candidate in a by-election for the Bengal Legislative Council,[1] and he himself in 1949 received twenty-eight Muslim votes in the Legislative Assembly as a candidate for the Central Legislature.

In spite of the existence of these elements of opposition, the achievement of the present Government in setting up the administration in a new capital, in balancing its budget and in preventing communal disturbances has been creditable. In the higher administrative services it was severely hampered by the almost total lack of Bengali Muslims in the Indian Civil Service; and the transfer of Bengali Hindu officers to India left most of the key positions in the secretariat in the hands of Punjabis and Muslims from the United Provinces.[2] It may be confidently predicted, however, that the presence in Karachi of a Governor General and Minister of the Interior, both of whom come from Bengal, will insure that the province obtains its fair share of future recruitment to the Pakistan services.

The place of East Bengal in Pakistan is the least easy of all the provinces to assess, and its future the most difficult to foresee. Flying from Karachi to Dacca, one passes from a dry country where the camel is the main means of transport, of tall

[1] East Bengal, unlike the other provinces of Pakistan, has an Upper House, the Legislative Council, in addition to the Legislative Assembly. It is elected on a much more restricted franchise than that of the latter.
[2] A rough estimate given to the writer in Dacca showed approximately twenty Muslims from outside the province, eight Englishmen, and two Bengal Muslims in the East Bengal cadre of the Pakistan Administrative Service in May 1949.

men with high cheek-bones, turbans and baggy trousers, to a country of huge rivers, where in the rains transport from village to village and house to house is by boat, where the men are short, broad-faced and bearded, and wear bright check lungis (skirts) and skull-caps. Western Pakistan is oriented towards the Middle East, Eastern Pakistan is irrevocably part of South East Asia. The Bengal Muslim is backward and isolated, living sometimes on islands which have never been charted, having perhaps no village teacher, unreached by radio or newspaper. Abductions of women and murders over land on the shifting river margin are frequent, and the fugitive can sometimes find asylum beyond the range of the law. The numbers are so great and the communications so poor that education can only advance slowly. Nor is the economic advance of the province certain, based as it is almost entirely on a single crop. For the establishment of local jute mills will be strongly opposed by vested interests from outside, and even the value of raw jute may be undermined by foreign substitutes. What seems certain in East Bengal, however, is that religion remains a very strong motive of social and political conduct, and that the further the suffrage is extended the more manifest this will be, and the less likely any political merger with India. The association between Western and Eastern Pakistan will, however, need to be nursed very carefully at both ends. It is unlikely to prove sufficient if it is only based on a common desire not to be a part of India. This seems recognized by the Central Government in the distribution of portfolios and appointments in Karachi. But perhaps nowhere in the world may the invention of the jet-propelled airliner, which should bring Dacca within three hours of Karachi, be of such vital importance in determining political history.

CHAPTER XI

Pakistan and India

Kashmir—Evacuee Property—Abducted Women—
Rivers—Inter-Dominion Agreements

Jinnah voiced the hope of every intelligent Pakistani when, on taking office as Governor General, he said that 'it will be our endeavour to create and maintain goodwill and friendship with our neighbouring Dominion'.[1] For India and Pakistan seemed united by common defence problems, by their economic inter-dependence and by the years of common service of their senior civil servants and soldiers. Yet their relationship has been a melancholy history. They have made bitter charges against each other before the United Nations. Their armies have fought against each other in Kashmir. No insult has been too petty for their Press to hurl across the border, and their statesmen have openly spoken of the possibility of war.

Far more than the Punjab massacres, which, though horrible, were short lived, it is the Kashmir dispute which has poisoned every aspect of Indo-Pakistan relations. The attitude of India and Pakistan to the question is quite different. To the educated Indian of Madras or Calcutta the Kashmir dispute is mainly a matter of prestige. His country is involved in a local quarrel with Pakistan, made spectacular by being carried on before the United Nations, and he patriotically hopes it will prevail. But it would make little material difference to his life if India

[1] Speech on 13th August 1947. *Speeches as Governor General*, p. 8.

did not obtain Kashmir. Indeed, some Indian businessmen have been doubtful in a time of inflation of the wisdom of spending so high a proportion of the national income in the struggle for an area deficit in food, and whose inhabitants' loyalty to India is questionable. Many of them would like to see the affair ended by any graceful compromise, irrespective of how much or little of Kashmir remained within the Dominion.

A glance at the map, on the other hand, will show what Kashmir means to Pakistan. The whole prosperity of Western Pakistan is dependent on her river and canal system. But of the five great rivers which irrigate the West Punjab and Sind, two, the Sutlej and Ravi, have their headwaters in India. The East Punjab Government has demanded seigniorage charges for the use of these waters in the Pakistan canals, and has claimed the right to divert them for its own use. The remaining three great rivers, the Indus, Jhelum and Chenab, have their headwaters in Kashmir. Their control by a hostile neighbour could mean ruin for Pakistan.

This is the aspect of the Kashmir dispute which weighs most heavily on the statesman and civil servant. But to the ordinary Pakistani, the spectacle of his brother Muslims in peril, described by local Press and radio as fighting with primitive weapons against the oppression of a tyrannical Hindu Maharajah and whole divisions of the Indian Army, has made the most striking appeal. The Azad Kashmir forces are referred to in the Press as 'crusaders'. Their leaders receive ovations greater than most Cabinet Ministers, and in the poorest areas of Pakistan enormous subscriptions have been collected for the expenses of the struggle. Senior Pakistan officials are told frankly by their barbers and tailors that the Government's support to the movement is too passive and niggardly. In April 1949 the *Civil and Military Gazette*, the oldest daily paper in Pakistan, had to be closed down by the Government for three months in Lahore, because popular opinion was so indignant at its suggestion that the Kashmir dispute was to be settled by partition.

Pakistan and India

The state of Jammu and Kashmir at the time of Partition was a huge and by no means homogeneous area, 78 per cent of whose population were Muslims, but ruled by a Hindu Maharajah, a Dogra Rajput whose ancestors had bought the greater part of the territory from the British East India Company in 1846. The state was divided into three provinces: Ladakh (or 'the Frontier Districts'), entirely mountainous and sparsely inhabited, 79 per cent of whose population were Muslims, with a Buddhist minority on the borders of Tibet; Kashmir Province, 93 per cent Muslim, containing the celebrated Valley whose craftsmen and cultivators were among the most impoverished and oppressed in India; and Jammu Province, 53 per cent Muslim,[1] containing good cultivable land in the east, but whose west was rocky and barren and a great recruiting ground for the Indian Army. Only in the three eastern districts of Jammu, south of the Chenab, was there a majority of Hindus and Sikhs.

The Maharajah's rule was autocratic and despotic. The incidence of the land revenue was treble that in the Punjab. The sale of grain was a state monopoly. There was a tax on every sheep, every hearth, and every wife, and a professional tax on butchers, bakers, carpenters, boatmen and even prostitutes. There was differential treatment of Muslims and Hindus. A Muslim, but not a Hindu, had to have a gun licence. A Hindu on conversion to Islam forfeited all interest in inherited property. The Muslims were beef eaters, but cow slaughter was punishable by a ten-year jail sentence.

The miserable condition of the people of the state was kept before the Indian public by a number of very distinguished Kashmiris whose families had settled in India. Thus Iqbal in 1932 warmly championed a revolt in Jammu against oppressive taxation, and Nehru in 1946, though a member of the Viceroy's Council, was arrested in Kashmir while supporting Sheikh Abdullah's 'Quit Kashmir' campaign against the Maharajah. There were two major political parties in the state: the National

[1] Percentages based on 1941 census figures. The Jammu percentage excludes Poonch, which was 90 per cent Muslim.

Conference, led by Sheikh Abdullah,[1] in general sympathy with the Indian National Congress; and the Muslim Conference, led by Choudhury Ghulam Abbas, which was allied to the All India Muslim League. At the time of Partition the leaders of both parties were in jail.

Kashmir's main roads, her only railway, and the rivers down which floated the timber which was her principal export, all led into Pakistan. At Partition, therefore, the Maharajah signed a Standstill Agreement with Pakistan by which the latter continued to run the posts and telegraphs and the railway, hitherto maintained by the Government of undivided India. It was generally assumed in Pakistan that the Standstill Agreement would lead in due course to accession, for Kashmir's only territorial link with India was an unmetalled road from Jammu to the East Punjab, and in winter no road could be kept open out of the Kashmir Valley except that into Pakistan. Moreover, it seemed unlikely that the Maharajah could resist the wish of the great majority of his subjects who, as Muslims, might be presumed to share the feelings which their neighbours in the North West Frontier Province and the West Punjab had recently expressed in favour of accession to Pakistan.

A series of distinct but related violent events, however, brought about Kashmir's accession to India and armed conflict between India and Pakistan. The first occurred in Poonch, a craggy, barren jagir in the west of Jammu which had contributed 40,000 troops to the Indian Army in the war of 1939–45. Led by ex-soldiers, the Muslims of Poonch demonstrated at the end of August 1947 in favour of accession to Pakistan. When their meetings were fired on, they rose in open revolt against the Maharajah, raising the slogan of 'no taxation without representation', and set up their own 'Azad Kashmir Government' under the presidency of Sardar Mohammed Ibrahim, a local barrister. After a short, fierce struggle, in which there was little quarter on either side, they expelled the State Forces from the whole of

---

[1] Sheikh Abdullah, who is a Muslim, was originally a member of the Muslim Conference, but left it in 1938 to form the National Conference.

Poonch and Mirpur Districts, with the exception of a beleaguered garrison in Poonch Town. The non-Muslim population suffered severely in the course of these events.

At the same time, Hindu and Sikh refugees from the West Punjab were coming into Jammu, where there seems to have been an attempt on the part of certain officials of the State Government to convert the province into a non-Muslim majority area. From the end of September until the atrocities were checked by Indian control in November, Muslims were rounded up in the villages and in Jammu City itself and told by civil and military officials to depart to Pakistan. Both foot and motor convoys were ambushed and slaughtered on their way by well-armed Hindu and Sikh bands. Many thousands perished and over a hundred thousand had reached Sialkot in the West Punjab by early November.

In the middle of October 1947 a new element appeared on the scene. The tribesmen of the North West Frontier and of Afghanistan came down to the plains of the Punjab each winter to seek temporary employment in a less severe climate. This year, already incensed by tales of the massacres in the Punjab, they saw an opportunity of gaining both religious merit and rich booty in the civil war which was being waged between Muslims and Hindus in the southern part of the state. How far they were assisted by officials and ministers of the North West Frontier Province and West Punjab Governments is disputed, but from Peshawar they swept down the Kashmir Valley, which had hitherto been unaffected by communal disturbances, easily overpowering the State Forces, and, burning and plundering as they went, came within a few miles of the summer capital of Kashmir at Srinagar. On 26th October, the Maharajah, whose army by now hardly existed,[1] sent his accession to the Government of India, and asked for the urgent despatch of Indian troops. At the same time he asked Sheikh Abdullah, whom he had released from jail a few weeks earlier, to form an administration. Mount-

[1] In addition to losses suffered in action, its Muslim units had deserted to the 'Azad Kashmir Forces'.

batten, as Governor General of India, accepted the accession, but added that as soon as order had been restored it should be confirmed by a referendum to the people. Indian troops landed by air at Srinagar, and pushed the tribesmen back up the valley to Uri. In the western part of Jammu, however, they made little progress against the 'Azad Kashmir Forces', in an area ideally suited to guerrillas. In Gilgit, whose garrison controlled most of the huge, sparsely populated province of Ladakh, when news of the Maharajah's accession to India arrived there was a bloodless revolution. The Governor was imprisoned, and on the invitation of the Gilgit Scouts and of the local chieftains, Pakistan sent a Political Agent to take over the government.

The Pakistanis were appalled and furious at India's acceptance of the accession of Kashmir, which they had always, from the time of the Lahore Resolution in 1940, regarded as an essential part of Pakistan, both politically and economically. Jinnah and Liaquat could not, had they wished, have restrained the people of the West Punjab from giving aid and encouragement to the 'Azad Kashmir Forces' in their retreat before the Indian Army and Air Force. They steadfastly resisted the popular clamour for open armed intervention, however, and proposed to India that the fighting should be stopped through a joint proclamation by the Governor Generals of both Dominions, and that a plebiscite should then be held under joint control. But the indignation of Nehru, Prime Minister of India, was equally great. Himself a Kashmiri, he had seen the most beautiful part of his native valley ravaged by tribal raiders, with what he believed to be the approval and aid of Pakistan. India took up the legal position that Kashmir was now part of her territory, in which Pakistan had no concern. If there was to be a plebiscite, India would conduct it. In January 1948 she charged Pakistan before the Security Council of the United Nations with assisting tribesmen and other invaders to violate her sovereignty. Pakistan made countercharges, that India had been guilty of genocide in the East Punjab, had usurped Pakistan's sovereignty in Junagadh and had obtained the accession of Kashmir by fraud and violence.

Pakistan and India

The initial reaction of the Security Council was to treat both parties as equal claimants to Kashmir, but India, by withdrawing her delegation and exercising diplomatic pressure, swung opinion more in her favour in March. In April a resolution was passed which was satisfactory to neither party. It called for the withdrawal of Pakistani nationals and of tribesmen from the state and for a reduction of India's forces. A plebiscite to determine the ultimate destiny of the state was to be conducted by a Plebiscite Administrator nominated by the United Nations but appointed by the Government of Jammu and Kashmir. The latter was to be broadened into a coalition of the main parties in the state. A five-power Commission was sent out to offer its good offices in bringing about a settlement.

The Commission arrived in the subcontinent to find a deteriorating situation. In spring India had mounted a successful offensive against the 'Azad Kashmir Forces'. Pakistan, apprehensive of being overwhelmed by a further million refugees, and of finally losing any chance of possession of the state and control of its rivers, sent regular troops into Kashmir in April to block the Indian progress towards certain strategic points. Thus detachments of armies owing allegiance to the same king, and each headed in Delhi and Rawalpindi by a British Commander-in-Chief, were in action against each other. Both the Indian and Pakistan Governments managed to resist pressure from their extremists, and the fighting remained localized. But it was not until January 1949 that the Commission obtained a cease-fire. This was based upon the principle that, during a subsequent truce period, the Pakistan forces and the bulk of the Indian Army should be withdrawn from the state. The Jammu and Kashmir Government of Sheikh Abdullah would continue to administer the territory which it held. The territory held by the 'Azad Kashmir Government' would be administered by the 'local authorities under the surveillance of the Commission'. Before the plebiscite the final disposal of the 'Azad Kashmir Forces' on the one hand and of the remaining Indian and State Forces on the other would be determined by the Commission in consultation with the local authorities and the Government of India respectively. By the autumn of 1949, however, though the tribesmen had gone home, the two Governments had been unable to agree on the details of the troop withdrawals, and their armies remained facing each other across a cease-fire line demarcated and supervised by United Nations observers. South and east of this line, the administration of the Kashmir Valley and most of Jammu Province was carried on by Sheikh Abdullah's government in the name of the Maharaja as a territory of the Indian Union. The area to the west of it was administered by the 'Azad Kashmir Government'. To the north the greater part of Ladakh province was controlled by Pakistan's Political Agent at Gilgit, though India occupied Kargil and Leh.

Hitherto the only solution to the dispute which has been officially discussed is a plebiscite, but although India and Pakistan have agreed throughout on the principle of a plebiscite, they have not been able to agree on the circumstances under which it should take place. An alternative which has been rather wistfully suggested by some of Sheikh Abdullah's supporters is an independent Kashmir, guaranteed by its neighbours. This has not been taken very seriously by the parties to the dispute, for it would seem certain that in such an independent Kashmir the struggle for power would continue between the partisans of India and of Pakistan. A solution with rather more to commend it has sometimes been hinted at in the Indian Press—that of partition. The only principle on which partition could be carried out with any hope of success would be that which was applied in Bengal and in the Punjab—the accession of contiguous Muslim majority areas to Pakistan and of non-Muslim areas to India, taking the 1941 census figures as a basis. Such a division would give the three eastern districts of Jammu Province, Kathua, Udhampur and Jammu Districts, to India, and perhaps the Buddhist eastern area of Ladakh; the remainder to Pakistan. It would probably be opposed both by India, which would be reluctant to abandon Sheikh Abdullah in the Kashmir Valley, and by Pakistan, who would lose control of the river Chenab.

Pakistan and India

Pakistan is convinced that in a fair plebiscite, which included the votes of the refugees, 500,000 of whom are in her territory, Kashmir would accede to her. She is also convinced that Indian control of the Kashmir rivers could mean ruin for the West Punjab. No government therefore which gave way on the Kashmir question would be likely to remain in office in Pakistan for a day. Until the Kashmir dispute is settled, there is no prospect whatever of improved relations with India; and Pakistan's defence policy, her foreign policy and much of her economic policy will continue to be based on the assumption that India is a potential enemy.

Apart from Kashmir, the most controversial and delicate question which has been the subject of negotiation between the Dominions is that of Evacuee Property. The minorities in both parts of the Punjab fled for their lives in the autumn of 1947, taking little of their movable property with them, and having no time to arrange the disposal of land, houses or business property. Incoming refugees, for whom there was no other accommodation, were settled by the Provincial Governments on the vacant land or premises. Ever since, the rights of the evacuees to compensation have been the subject of conferences between the Dominions. In January 1949 an agreement was signed by which evacuees were entitled to receive rent for their urban property, or to sell or exchange it. The agreement was limited to Western Pakistan on the one hand and to East Punjab and the East Punjab states on the other, and the governments concerned were entitled to requisition residential establishments for three years and industrial establishments for five years, on payment of rent. The agreement has not worked well. In Pakistan, prospective buyers have been discouraged because the premises were not available for immediate occupation, and there has been a wide gap between prices asked and prices offered. Recently, Pakistan has accused India of unilaterally extending the arrangement to include urban property in Bombay and the United Provinces. India has accused Pakistan of confiscating the property of non-Muslims who are still living in Pakistan. No agreement has been reached on the rights of evacuees in agricultural property.

Another legacy of the Punjab disturbances has been the recovery of the women who were abducted on both sides in 1947. This has naturally aroused acute feeling among their relatives. Social workers on both sides have worked hard to trace and restore the women. According to a statement issued by the Government of India on 30th July 1949,[1] a total of 11,251 Muslim women had been recovered in India up to 27th June, whereas 5,846 Hindu and Sikh women had been recovered in Pakistan. The Indians maintain that the figures show that the Pakistanis have been less active in the work of restoration. The Pakistanis maintain that on the contrary this only supports their claim that far fewer women were abducted in Pakistan than in India. Undoubtedly many women on both sides have died, leaving no record, but are still being sought indignantly by their relatives, and until the operation is concluded it will continue to be the subject of recriminations.

Recently,[2] quite apart from the Kashmir dispute, Pakistan has hinted that she may appeal to the Security Council to settle her disagreement with India over the waters of the Ravi, Sutlej and Beas rivers, which flow from the East Punjab into the West Punjab. Pakistan's point of view is that she has a right, generally acknowledged in international law, to continue to use these waters for irrigation. India's case[3] is that far less of the East Punjab is under canal irrigation than of the West Punjab, and that it is essential for the former to tap these rivers and bring new land under cultivation in order to settle the Hindu and Sikh refugees, many of whom come from the canal colonies of the West Punjab. Pakistan's attitude in this dispute is embittered by the memory that the water supply of Lahore was in fact cut off suddenly for a few weeks by the East Punjab Government in April 1948.

[1] Published in *Statesman*, weekly edition, 6th August 1949.

[2] 'Spokesman of Pakistan Foreign Office', reported in *Statesman*, weekly edition, 10th September 1949.

[3] As stated by the Minister for Works of India, September 1949, *India Record*, 22nd September 1949.

Pakistan and India

The most successful Inter-Dominion Conferences have been those conducted by civil servants and technicians, rather than ministers, on either side. A common set of customs rules has been approved, as well as conventions on the searching of transit passengers and the through transport of goods. Mutual facilities for the repairs of railway rolling stock have been arranged. Inter-Dominion agreements for the supply of raw materials by Pakistan to India and of manufactured goods by India to Pakistan have not worked badly[1] in spite of mutual suspicion and occasional public recrimination.

The Calcutta Conference of April 1948, at which Ghulam Mohammed led Pakistan's delegation, laid down some important political principles. It was agreed that the minorities in both Dominions should have full political, cultural, economic and religious rights; that the responsibility of protecting them rested on the Government of the Dominion in which they reside; and that provincial minority boards should be set up in West and East Bengal to safeguard their interests. The Premier and Chief Secretaries of West and East Bengal would hold monthly meetings to discuss minority questions. Each Dominion pledged itself to discourage propaganda in favour of 'the amalgamation of India and Pakistan or of portions thereof', and to restrain its Press from attacking the other Dominion. In the Delhi Conference of December 1948, it was agreed that a tribunal should be set up to settle minor boundary disputes between the provinces.

The minutes of the Inter-Dominion Conference held in Delhi in April 1949, show that in spite of very strained political relations, negotiations over a wide range of minor matters arising from partition continue to be conducted in a rational spirit. The Conference appointed thirteen subcommittees, and in the course of three days reached agreement on the payment of pensions to displaced persons, the transfer of cash certificates, the division of museum exhibits, of the survey of India assets, and of civil aviation equipment, the co-ordination of wireless

[1] Until the devaluation of September 1949. But see p. 194 below.

frequencies and on a joint machinery for the prevention of border raids. Useful consultations took place on many other subjects, which were referred back to the Governments for further consideration.

There is no doubt that among educated Indians and Pakistanis, politicians, civil servants and educationalists, even in the Punjab, where many lost relations and property in 1947, there is realization that the prosperity of their countries can only be built on friendship with the other Dominion. They know that over the past two years they have frequently stood on the verge of war, and that war between India and Pakistan would be disastrous for both, and helpful only to Communism. But there is this difference on the two sides of the border: educated Pakistanis believe that war would be no more catastrophic to their economy than the loss of Kashmir, whereas many educated Indians would consider India better off politically and economically without Kashmir but with Pakistan's friendship. Without forming a judgment on the legal rights of the case, it may be stated that the Kashmir dispute is only likely to be settled and friendship between the Dominions assured if India, which has so much less to lose, feels able to make a generous gesture.

CHAPTER XII

Foreign Policy and Defence

*Pakistan's Neighbours—Friction with Afghanistan—
Sympathy with Muslims of the Middle East—Deteriora-
ting Relations with Britain and the Commonwealth—
U.S.A.—Russia—The Army, Navy and Air Force—
British Personnel in the Services.*

There have been two main factors in Pakistan's foreign policy, firstly her geographical position, especially her contiguity to India; secondly, her feeling of kinship with other Muslim countries, particularly those of the Middle East. The first of these considerations has mainly shaped her relationship to the British Commonwealth; the second has guided her spokesmen in the deliberations of the United Nations, of which she became a member in September 1947.

Western Pakistan is bounded by Iran, Afghanistan, India and the Arabian Sea. *De facto* control of the northern areas of Kashmir brings her territory also to the borders of the Sinkiang Province of China, and within twelve miles of the U.S.S.R. Eastern Pakistan is bounded by India, Burma and the Bay of Bengal. Of these neighbours, relations with Burma are cordial and those with Iran excellent, being strengthened by cultural ties. The civil war has delayed diplomatic representation in China. An exchange of ambassadors with the U.S.S.R. has been agreed, and it has been announced that Liaquat Ali is to make a goodwill visit to Moscow.

Foreign Policy and Defence

Relations with Afghanistan, the only nation which opposed Pakistan's entry into the United Nations, have not been happy. The Kabul radio and Press have repeatedly urged the tribes on the Pakistan side of the Durand Line to rise and create an independent 'Pathanistan'. The Afghan Government has supported the Press campaign by distributing presents to the tribesmen. Pakistan has few apprehensions as to the loyalty of the latter, whose standard of living is higher than that on the other side of the Frontier, and has no fear of the ill-paid Afghan Army. But many Pakistanis suspect Indian intrigue and money behind this movement in an effort to divert tribal interest from Kashmir.[1] The Afghan dynasty is believed to be precariously balanced between the attacks of Communists on the one hand and those of supporters of the family of ex-King Amanullah on the other, and to be attempting to save itself by concentrating attention on external rather than internal affairs. In June 1949 the Afghan Government alleged that a Pakistan aeroplane had bombed a village within her territory. Pakistan promptly accepted the findings of a joint Commission which established the responsibility of a Pakistan Air Force plane for the accidental bombing, and offered full compensation, but the settlement of this incident has led to no diminution of the Afghan propaganda.

Ceylon is not a neighbour, but is important as providing port facilities along the line of sea communications between Western and Eastern Pakistan. Relations between the two Dominions appear to have been harmonious.

Pakistan's sympathy with other Muslim nations has been ably expressed at the General Assembly of the United Nations by her Foreign Minister, Sir Mohammad Zafrullah Khan, who has been described by the American representative, Senator Warren Austin, as 'One of our greatest statesmen. Whether addressing formal meetings or participating in informal conversations, he is always just and fair'.[2] Both on the question of Palestine and the

---

[1] No evidence of Indian complicity has, however, been published.
[2] In the General Assembly of the United Nations, 2nd May 1949.

disposal of the Italian colonies in Africa, Zafrullah contributed the clearest and most persuasive statement of the Arab case. On the latter question he led the smaller nations in a remarkable success in defeating the proposal of the Western Powers to hand back Libya to Italy. His strong but unsuccessful opposition to the partition of Palestine was backed by a speech by Liaquat Ali in Karachi who said: 'In the case of resumption of hostilities in Palestine, we must despatch contingents of Razakars and Muja- hids.'[1]

Pakistan has joined India in consistent support for the Indo- nesian Republic against the Dutch, and refused transit facilities to Dutch shipping and aircraft during 1948–9. Zafrullah has also frequently expressed sympathy for the people of Indo-China and of Malaya in their desire for self-government.

The earliest permanent diplomatic missions which Pakistan set up after independence, apart from those in Britain and the U.S.A., were embassies in Egypt, Iran, Afghanistan and Turkey. All these countries, as well as Iraq, Saudi Arabia and Trans- jordan have representatives in Karachi. The Education Ministry has sponsored Pakistan-Iran, Pakistan-Afghan, Pakistan-Arab and Pakistan-Turkish Associations in the capital. In announcing this step, the Education Minister said:

'With these countries we claim a community of outlook based on spiritual and moral affinities. We have the same faith and the same cultural traditions as they have, and, like us, they too are emerging from the sloth of centuries and are becoming increas- ingly conscious of the important historical role which Islam has to play as a world-unifying force. It is therefore natural that our first cultural links should be with them.'

But there is another cultural association which Pakistan has, whether willingly or unwillingly, inherited; that with Britain and the Commonwealth. Her legal institutions are based on English law. Her form of government is modelled on parliamentary practice. Her armed forces are trained by British officers and

[1] Quoted from *Dawn*, 11th September 1948. 'Razakars' may be freely translated as 'Volunteers', and 'Mujahids' as 'Crusaders'.

have British uniforms and equipment. English is still the language of her universities and of her most influential newspapers. At the time of Partition, there was a great fund of goodwill for Britain. Jinnah, on assuming office as Governor General, stated: 'Such voluntary and absolute transfer of power and rule by one nation over others is unknown in the history of the world. It is the translation and realization of the Great Ideal of Commonwealth which now has been effected; and hence both Pakistan and Hindustan have remained members of the Commonwealth, which shows how truly we appreciate the high and noble ideal by which the Commonwealth has been and will be guided in the future.'[1] British officers were appointed as Governors of three of the four provinces and as heads of the armed services: and Britain was asked to help in setting up the new foreign office and in supplying technicians, teachers and capital. The Commonwealth, many Pakistanis felt, was a family in which Britain as the eldest brother could be relied upon to give sound advice to Pakistan as the youngest member.

In this spirit Pakistan appealed to Britain and the Commonwealth in October 1947 to help restore order in the Punjab, at least by sending neutral observers. The answer she received from the British Government was so coldly phrased that she took it as a snub. At about the same time the British Supreme Commander who had been looked to by Pakistan to ensure the despatch of her fair share of the war material from the stores of undivided India, was withdrawn, leaving most of his task uncompleted. Then came the dispute with India over Kashmir. At the Security Council the British delegate was expected to give a lead by members of the Council who made no secret of their imperfect knowledge of a remote part of Asia. To the Pakistanis it seemed that initially the British and Canadian delegates treated the problem fairly on its merits, and suggested a solution not unfavourable to Pakistan; but that subsequently India successfully applied diplomatic pressure, particularly on the British Government,

[1] Speech at banquet in honour of Lord Mountbatten, 13th August 1947. *Speeches as Governor General*, p. 7.

with a result that the April resolution of the Security Council proposed the creation of a plebiscite machinery heavily weighted in her favour.

Throughout the Kashmir fighting the Commonwealth made no overt sign of intervention. Arms were supplied to both sides, though British officers were not allowed into the fighting area. Shortly after the cease-fire, Air Vice-Marshal Elmhirst, who commanded the Royal Indian Air Force, was reported by the Indian Press as stating that India was receiving more up-to-date types of aircraft from the United Kingdom than was Pakistan. This confirmed the impression of the Pakistan Government that their needs were consistently being subordinated to those of India, and that India had friends in the British Labour Party who would always be influential enough to cause the Cabinet to side with India in an important dispute with Pakistan. They read and were irritated by the references of British ministers[1] and Imperial commentators[2] to 'India's position of leadership in South East Asia'. But they were comforted by the knowledge that Congress leaders were pledged to make India a republic, and were confident that when India left the Commonwealth Pakistan's loyalty would be better appreciated.

At the Commonwealth Prime Ministers' Conference of April 1949, however, it was agreed that India, when she became a republic, should remain within the Commonwealth. Liaquat Ali, who attended the Conference on behalf of Pakistan, was moved to warn the London Press that Pakistan 'could not be taken for granted' and 'treated like a camp follower'. Although his warning was mildly phrased, it brought to boiling point an indignation which had been simmering for months among Pakistani politicians and newspapermen. *Dawn*, the Muslim League

[1] e.g., Sir Stafford Cripps, quoted in London *Times* of 9th July 1949, as saying that 'the stability of the Asiatic world, which was threatened on every side, depended largely on the leadership of India', in an address to the Indian Merchants Bureau in London.

[2] e.g., Professor N. Mansergh, Abe Bailey Professor of British Commonwealth Relations: 'India . . . has by virtue of her geographical position and her capacity for leadership in South East Asia, wider responsibilities to perform.' *The Commonwealth and the Nations*, London, 1948, p. 160.

Karachi daily paper, demanded that 'British elements should be eliminated from civilian administrative positions and from those positions in the armed forces for which Pakistani substitutes could be found. . . . Even for those positions in which foreigners must be appointed because suitable Pakistani personnel are lacking, search should first be made elsewhere than in the British Isles.'[1] Within a few weeks Sir Ambrose Dundas, Governor of the North West Frontier Province, and Sir Francis Mudie, Governor of the West Punjab, had resigned, the latter after bitter onslaughts directed against him by the Press and the Provincial Muslim League. Both Governors were replaced by Pakistanis. Liaquat Ali, on his return from London, announced that he would pay a courtesy visit to Moscow in the autumn.

It is difficult not to conclude that the British Government has been unimaginative in its dealings with Pakistan. The first mistake was, perhaps, to allow Mountbatten to continue after the Partition as Governor General of India. It had been suggested that he should remain as Governor General of both Dominions. The Muslim League, however, pointed out that this arrangement would be unworkable. For whereas the Governor General must have the confidence of his Cabinet and must act on its advice, a situation might arise in which information must be kept from the other Dominion, or in which a policy which was not agreeable to the other Dominion had to be stated. Jinnah urged therefore that each Dominion should have its own Governor General, but that Mountbatten should remain as Agent of the Crown to supervise the disposal of India's assets. This advice was not accepted. Mountbatten remained as Governor General of the Indian Dominion, and it is no criticism of him to say that he worked hard in its interests in negotiations with the States and with Pakistan. Pakistanis, however, bitterly resented his acceptance of the accession of Kashmir, and tribesmen and 'Azad Kashmir Forces' spoke of the planes which bombed them as 'sent by Mountbatten, who was once our

[1] *Dawn*, Karachi, 8th May 1949.

171

Commander in Burma'.[1] Yet at the same time he had to serve as 'neutral Chairman' of the Joint Defence Council, and remained bound by whatever assurances of fair treatment he had given to the Muslim League leaders when they accepted Partition. The Pakistanis were convinced that his advice continued to carry the same weight with the British Cabinet now that he was a partisan of India as it had when he was Viceroy.

Much more fundamental than personalities has been the different conception of the Commonwealth held by the British and Pakistan Governments. The British attitude has been that the Commonwealth can exert no pressure on either India or Pakistan to stop fighting in Kashmir, and to settle the dispute. Tactfully ignoring the fact that the armies of both Dominions are concentrated against each other, it has preferred to discuss joint defence against a potential external aggressor, presumably Russia, a defence apparently to be organized under Indian leadership.

The Pakistan point of view is that if the Commonwealth cannot settle its own disputes, if it cannot guarantee one member against aggression by another, then its membership is of little importance. Pakistan feels her very existence menaced by India. It would be admirable if she could be convinced that her fears are groundless, but to offer her instead protection against Afghanistan, whose army she regards as puny, or a defence pact against Russia, with whom she has no quarrel, is to avoid the main issue. As for 'Indian Leadership in South East Asia', Pakistan's reaction to such a project might be gauged from her refusal to be included in any agency of the United Nations which has its headquarters in Delhi, and from her reluctance to place the interests of Pakistani nationals under Indian protection in any of the countries where she has herself no consular services. In an interesting paper on 'The Commonwealth, India and Pakistan', Mr. K. Sarwar Hasan, Secretary of the Pakistan Institute of International Affairs, has recently stated bluntly what the Pakistan Government has to hint more delicately.

[1] Reported in Calcutta *Statesman*, 2nd March 1948; and London *Daily Mail*, 17th November 1947.

Foreign Policy and Defence

'The people of Pakistan would like . . . assurances given of active intervention on her side in the event of aggression by India, as much as that by Russia. The people of Pakistan would also like to be assured that the state that is externally associated would in no sense be treated more favourably by the Commonwealth than a state which is a full member of it. Unless these assurances are forthcoming, and are acted upon, Pakistan would have no interest in the Commonwealth.'[1]

Alienation from Britain has to some extent inclined Pakistan to look to America for friendship and assistance. The nomination of Admiral Nimitz as Kashmir Plebiscite Administrator was warmly welcomed, and *Dawn* has recommended that American technicians should be recruited in place of Englishmen. But despite the energetic work of their Ambassador in the U.S.A., M. A. H. Ispahani, a progressive young businessman, Pakistanis realize that the influence of their country in America is slight by comparison with that of India. They recollect that when Jinnah died, most of the American journals drew their obituary information from Indian sources. Ever since the triumphant appearance of Swami Vivekananda at the Chicago Parliament of Faiths, Hinduism has been a subject of great interest in America, certainly of far wider interest than Islam; and the American friendships of Mr. Gandhi and the diligent work of the 'India League' have made the leaders of the Indian Congress familiar to most American newspaper readers. Perhaps such factors have no great weight in shaping American policy, but so closely is that policy linked with that of Britain in South East Asia that Pakistanis feel that it is most unlikely that the United States will diverge from what appears to be the British plan of basing the defence of the area on Indian leadership.

If, then, neither Britain nor America is willing to guarantee Pakistan's borders and existence against India, and if she remains obsessed by the danger of attack from India, it is inevitable that she should reflect on her relationship with the third

[1] K. Sarwar Hasan, *The Commonwealth, India and Pakistan*, Pakistan Institute of International Affairs, Karachi, June 1949.

great power. Russia abstained from voting on the Kashmir question in the Security Council, and has given no indication of her sympathies in the area. Ideologically, the Pakistan Government and the Muslim League are strongly opposed to Communism; nowhere in South East Asia perhaps are its native forces less strong and the ground less fertile for its growth. But in the last resort, if it came to a war with India in which Pakistan's back would be against the wall of the Himalayas, many Pakistanis have told the writer that religious sentiment would completely outweigh economic considerations; that an emotional fear of Hindu domination would obliterate apprehensions of the consequences of a Marxist regime; and that help would be sought from behind the mountain wall if it were not available from the Western powers. No one who has lived in and has friendships both in India and Pakistan can talk lightly of war between them, but it would be foolish to ignore the fact that they have been very close to war in the past two years. And it is against this background that Liaquat Ali's visit to Moscow has been welcomed in Pakistan, even by those classes which would have most to lose under Communism.

Pakistan's defence policy has naturally been influenced by her foreign policy. At Partition she took over about 150,000 troops and airmen out of a total of 420,000 in the Indian Army and Air Force. Had the country remained undivided, it was intended to reduce this strength by about half.[1] In fact, although no figures are now published, it seems clear that Pakistan's defence services have been considerably expanded.

The army on Partition had to be hastily assembled from all parts of India and used to protect refugee camps and convoys, at a time when many of the officers and men concerned were ignorant of the fate of their own families. No sooner had the Punjab evacuation been completed than fighting started in Kashmir. The Pakistan units which were sent into the state were given a very delicate task. They were instructed to guard certain

[1] Sir Archibald Rowlands in *Royal Central Asian Journal*, vol. xxxv, 1948.

key points, but not to take any initiative. They were bombed, but had no air support. For several months their presence was a secret, so that they had no moral backing from the Press, radio, or from home letters. Their morale, however, was high, sustained by a crusading zeal for the protection of brother Muslims and a conviction that the existence of Pakistan depended on their efforts.

The army profited in two respects from its participation in the Kashmir war. Firstly, since British officers were not allowed in the fighting area, a correspondingly greater responsibility devolved on to Pakistani officers, and plans for nationalization were thus accelerated. Secondly, valuable experience was gained of co-operation with tribal lashkars, several of which had previously fought against the (British) Indian Army. The withdrawal of the army from the tribal areas in the autumn of 1947 had created goodwill which was confirmed by the joint operations in Kashmir, where the tribesmen carried out the general directions of the Pakistan Army under the tactical leadership of their own Maliks. It is lamentable that such experience should have had to be gained against India, but it may prove to have been a very useful training if Pakistan is ever attacked on her northern frontier.

In Eastern Pakistan border defence is complicated by the difficulty of maintaining communications across huge rivers and through jungle and paddy fields. These are, of course, obstacles to an invader also, but are by no means insuperable, as was proved in the Burma War of 1941–5. The Bengalis, though contributing excellent seamen to the Navy, seldom entered the Indian Army before Partition. Pakistan has recruited an army brigade in Bengal, but it is too early to estimate its value. The bulk of the Pakistan Army is composed of Punjabi Muslims, Pathans and Baluchis, with a strong element of Poonchis from Western Kashmir. As a second line of defence, when relations with India began to deteriorate in 1947, a Pakistan National Guard was raised. This consists of unpaid volunteers who attend a fixed number of parades each year and who can be mobilized in an emergency. Originally the recruitment target was twenty-four battalions, but the response was so enthusiastic that by July 1948 fifty-four battalions had been raised in addition to a Women's Wing.

The army at Partition was particularly short of artillery and engineer officers, and of technicians of all branches. It was further handicapped by having to start new schools of instruction, the majority of these being in India. A Pakistan military academy, a school for military engineers and other training institutes have been set up; and officers have been sent to Britain and America for advanced training, but it seems likely that foreign technical instructors and advisers will have to be employed even after the army as a whole has been nationalized.

A coast line of nearly 1,000 miles is one of Pakistan's most formidable defence problems. The Navy took over at Partition eight ships and eight small craft with a total strength of 180 officers and 3,400 ratings. Two destroyers have since been purchased from Britain. Excellent training establishments already existed in Karachi and another is being established at Chittagong. Recruiting has been successful both in Western and Eastern Pakistan, and a Reserve Fleet has been created.

The Royal Pakistan Air Force consisted at Partition of two fighter squadrons, a transport squadron, an air observation post flight, and a communications flight. A flying training school was established at Risalpur in 1947, and there has been considerable expansion of the R.P.A.F. Additional fighters have been purchased from Britain, but the acquisition of heavier types of aircraft has been delayed by the refusal of the U.S.A. to supply armaments either to India or Pakistan during the Kashmir fighting. The R.P.A.F. took no direct part in the Kashmir War, but its achievement in keeping communications open to Gilgit throughout has required skilful flying among the highest mountains in the world. British personnel have been supplemented by Polish officers and N.C.O.s demobilized from the R.A.F., who are employed both as instructors and for operational duties.

In May 1949 there were still approximately 350 British officers